DAIRE BRUN

G000075745

THE WARTIME
IRISH
MARINE
SERVICE

THE FIRST-HAND EXPERIENCES OF BROADCASTER
NORRIS DAVIDSON

The History Press

First published 2023

The History Press
97 St George's Place, Cheltenham,
Gloucestershire, GL50 3QB
www.thehistorypress.co.uk

British Library Cataloguing in Publication Data.
A catalogue record for this book is available from the British Library.

ISBN 978 1 80399 172 6

Typesetting and origination by The History Press
Printed and bound in Great Britain by TJ Books Limited, Padstow, Cornwall.

Trees for LYfe

Contents

Foreword

The Marine Service 1939–46

I was in contact with Norris Davidson
over several years – many years ago now –
when researching my book *The Seahound,*
the history of the famous *Muirchu.* He
was always most forthcoming with information and extracts from his diary for
the period. I only met him briefly once
when he did a radio documentary on
'Sea Sunday' in Cobh, sometime in the
1980s. He gave his unpublished manuscript *Various Courses* into my care and
this is now seeing the light of day. The
original manuscript is in the care of
Defence Forces Archives in Cathal Brugha
Barracks (Portobello Barracks) in Dublin,
where Norris was first enlisted into the
Defence Forces.

Norris in the Officer Training Corps
at Portora School, Enniskillen.

Norris joining the Irish Defence Forces is mildly surprising. People of his
class and background in that era in Ireland tended to gravitate towards the
British armed forces. He was in the Officer Training Corps (OTC) while at
school at Portora Royal School in Enniskillen. This taught military disciplines
and leadership. While not constituting an army reserve force, it obviously
pointed boys towards British military careers. His later education at Cambridge
was also consistent with the general trend of young men of his class at that
period. However, it is quite clear from his writing that there was no ambiguity

in where his loyalties lay. The 'Volunteers' that Norris joined initially in Portobello Barracks was an army part-time reserve. It had a uniform distinctive from the regular army (see centre illustrations). It disappeared sometime in the 1939–45 period with the formation of the Local Defence Force (LDF), which in turn was reorganised and renamed as the Fórsa Cosanta Áituil (FCA) and is now the Army Reserve.

When war broke out in Europe in September 1939, Ireland was one of the least prepared countries to deal with the consequences. The army had suffered years of political and financial neglect; worse, the Defence Vote had been constantly chipped away in successive budgets. This resulted in an army reduced in numbers, lacking any modern weapons, virtually no air defence and no seaward defence. Whatever the status of the army and the air corps, the lack of any seaward defence was a result of a national 'sea blindness', which also affected the fishing industry and the mercantile marine. Also, the terms of the Anglo-Irish Treaty of 1921 prohibited the Irish Free State having a navy until agreement had been made with the 'Imperial Government' about the form of such a force. A meeting took place in 1927 in London, but no agreement was reached and the status quo remained where the defence of Irish waters remained the responsibility of the British navy and the British army in the harbour defence forts in Cork Harbour, Berehaven and Lough Swilly. This situation continued until 1938, when the forts were handed over to the Irish state with great fanfare and publicity, and the Royal Navy departed from Irish waters, almost unnoticed. The army high command had drawn up an outline for an Irish naval force, but little action had been taken when war broke out in Europe in September 1939.

Royal Navy destroyer approaching her mooring, Cobh, 1936.

It was soon realised that to remain neutral and to comply with the terms of the Hague Convention for a neutral state in time of war, such a state had to have armed ships commanded by commissioned officers to deny the use of its waters and harbours to belligerents. Ireland had neither armed ships nor officers.

Earlier in 1939 the administrative cadre and outline of a Marine and Coast Watching Service had been set up by the army, and the Coast Watching part was quickly brought into being in September, establishing lookout posts on headlands around the east and south coasts, and later all around the coasts of the state. Two motor torpedo boats (M.T.Bs) had been ordered from a firm in England, but construction had not even started when war broke out. No structure existed for manning and man-aging such vessels, although advertisements appeared in the papers for people

Department of Agriculture Research and Patrol vessel *Muirchu*, 1936.

with sea experience and qualifications to apply for service in the defence forces in an, as yet, undefined structure.

The two vessels operated by the Department of Agriculture and Fisheries for research and fishery protection, the ageing *Muirchu* and chartered deep-sea trawler *Fort Rannoch*, were taken up by the Department of Defence in December 1939. They were each fitted with a 12-pdr gun, a couple of Vickers machine guns, radio, and painted grey. They were described as 'Public Armed Ships' and their crews were commissioned and enlisted into the defence forces. Meanwhile, the people recruited in response to the advertisement in the papers were accommodated in Collins Barracks in Dublin and training was started in military disciplines and certain maritime activities.

The order for motor torpedo boats was increased to six. There were two under construction for Baltic states that had been overrun by the Soviet Union, and these, being near completion, were sold to Ireland. The first, designated *M.1*, was commissioned in London by the Irish High Commissioner John Dulanty in January 1940 and arrived in Dublin in March that year. During the evacuation of the British Expeditionary Force from Dunkirk, the second M.T.B, *M.2*, nearing completion, was taken over by the British navy to assist. The Irish Marine Service officer Lt Billy Richardson (see p8 of plate section), standing by the new vessel, went with it. In the event it only got to Dover, ready to evacuate some VIPs from Dunkirk, but it wasn't used and returned to the yard for completion. *M.3*, on her passage down the English Channel in June 1940 on her way to Ireland, was attacked by German aircraft. Two bombs narrowly missed the vessel, causing minor damage. There were no casualties and she was escorted into nearby Portland by British M.T.Bs. Repairs were carried out and she resumed her passage to Cork Harbour.

These M.T.Bs were fast small (75ft) attack craft. Their main armament was their two torpedoes in tubes on either side of the vessels. Their main defence was their small size and their speed of over 30 knots. They initially were armed with a Madsen gun each, later replaced by a smaller AA weapon. They also carried four depth charges and a hydrophone to listen for submarines. Four massive 12-cylinder petrol engines provided the main power. These were paired to connect to two propellor shafts. The hulls were of diagonal mahogany planking, hard chine, meaning largely flat bottomed, so that at full speed they planed on the sea surface. They were only practical in calm to moderate sea condition, so they were not suitable for patrol work, although they were initially used in this role.

This, then was the naval force facing likely invasion in 1940 and 1941: two small patrol vessels and three M.T.Bs. The derelict naval dockyard on Haulbowline Island was taken over in the summer of 1940 as a base for this tiny fleet. Considerable work was done by army engineers, the Board of Works, the Construction Corps and the men of the Marine Service itself to bring the place up to some degree of use and habitability, including the necessary engineering and technical support for the highly sophisticated engines of the M.T.Bs. The remaining three M.T.Bs arrived in 1942. Some other supporting craft were also acquired: some launches, a small cargo steamer

M.T.B on patrol, Dunmore East.

used to set up defensive minefields and a three-masted schooner as a training ship.

Training vessel *Isaalt*.

The Marine Service was supported by a part-time reserve called the Maritime Inscription. Units of this were established in the main ports, providing a defensive element and conducting the inspection of shipping entering. They wore the same uniform as the Marine Service. After the 'Emergency' the number of units was reduced and the organisation was incorporated as a reserve unit of the Defence Forces and named 'An Slúa Muiri'. This in due course was renamed the Naval Reserve.

The invasion never came, but the war was all around Ireland in those years. The lookout posts reported attacks on convoys by German submarines and aircraft, of burning ships, of boats of survivors arriving on the coasts, corpses and other tragic results of the war at sea. German aircraft overflew Irish airspace with impunity, attacking shipping and fishing vessels in Irish waters. Several Irish ships were sunk with loss of life. The Marine Service patrol vessels patrolled dangerous waters over those years, establishing Irish sovereignty in its territorial seas and harbour and dealing with the practicalities such as rescuing survivors, dealing with derelicts and investigating and reporting on suspicious activities.

One of the most dangerous duties for the Marine Service was disposing of floating mines. The British had laid huge minefields to the south of Ireland against German submarines. In such exposed and stormy waters these mines frequently broke adrift and drifted into Irish coastal waters and onto the shore. For example, in the early hours of one morning, the seaman on duty on the patrol vessel *Muirchu* anchored in Glandore Harbour saw a mine alongside the ship. He had to fend it off with a boathook while calling for help, and while a boat was launched. It was duly towed carefully out to sea, where it could be safely disposed of. The mines that grounded were dealt with by Army Ordnance Corps people, those at sea by the Marine Service (see Chapter 6). The procedure was to get close enough to get a reasonable chance of hitting the mine by rifle fire, but far enough off to give some degree of safety if the mine exploded, which it frequently did. When it did, the ship would get a considerable shock and those on deck were in danger from falling shrapnel. More often the mine sank when enough bullet holes were punched into the casing. For years afterwards mines were brought up in fishing nets, occasionally with tragic results. There were several hundred mines disposed of by the army and the Marine Service.

With the end of the war, the Marine Service was reduced to about 160 all ranks, almost half its full complement. Morale was poor mainly due to a complete lack of appreciation or acknowledgement of its role, its ethos and its successes. Norris illustrates this very well in the final chapter and the bitterness that spoiled what should have been a recognition of heroic efforts and achievements.

The positive outcome was that it proved the necessity of maintaining an Irish naval force and decisions were made to establish a naval element as part of the Permanent Defence Forces. In 1946 the Naval Service was established, building on the foundations of the wartime Marine Service. The navy celebrates this date as its birthday, but its real beginning was in the turbulent days of 1939–40, where the 'can do' ethos was established. This book is a small tribute to those heroes, like Norris, who manned the pathetic little fleet and were prepared to be the first to challenge any invader or incursion into Irish territory.

I have changed almost nothing in Norris's book, just some minor typos; for example, he would write 'did'nt' instead of 'didn't' which I found strange, and maybe he was more correct.

Norris's relations, Simon Curthoys and Nik and Norry Boulting, were most helpful in the preparation of this book, for which I am most grateful, and likewise Commandant Daniel Ayiotis of Defence Forces Archives and Penny Fitzpatrick of Tighfitz, where Norris stayed in Aran. David Jones, as always, was most forthcoming with images from the Naval Photographic Archive.

Daire Brunicardi

Landing craft found abandoned off the west coast.

Various Courses

By Norris Davidson

W.O. Norris Davidson.
No.1 Patrol Vessel
c/o Marine Service COBH

1

Slipped

After reading the Synge book for the first time, a friend and I brooded over a six-inch map of the islands in the library of the Union Society Cambridge and it ended up by his coming home with me in the Long Vacation and our proceeding to the islands with a tent. I returned with that tent several times and then storms began to tear it, and I wearied of cooking and washing up and cooking again and so I took up my final abode in Patrick Fitzpatrick's public house in Killeany, near the eastern end of Inismor. There I sleep over the bar in a double-bed with a spring mattress of the tension I like. A wooden wash-hand and a dressing-table, a chair and a holy picture and a few goat-skin rugs on the floor and there you have the room in which I have so often and so long lain listening to the wind and the driving rain, or watching the sun making the limestone rocks on the hillside opposite shimmer in the heat. Opposite the bar and opening into the kitchen is my sitting-room; a lot of family photographs, an oleagraph of a pope, the Infant Jesus of Prague, headless and holding up the window, a dresser, a table, a wicker chair and a little French harmonium on whose repair I have spent many a wet day.

The house is square and faced with mortar, the kind of house a child might draw with so many windows and so many doors and a chimney at either end with smoke going up. Yes it is

Fitzpatrick's public house. Davidson's room is the upper window on the right.

the square house a child draws from exactly in front, possibly adding the unseen gable in the Chinese manner, and at its back is a cliff and the sea.

In that island, Inismor; in that village Killeany; in and around that house, I was spending part of every year, any part of the year seemed equally good. I have always been happy there, how, it would be hard to say. Lying on the grass soaking up the sun and listening to the larks; fishing off the Glassan Rocks; sailing, or walking along the cliffs during a storm or I might be sitting near the fire in my visiting house each evening, talking or listening as I pleased, or catching mackerel from my boat, or in Mr Daly's public-house – that low wonderful white-washed pub where you get the best pint in the world. It's a very hard pub to leave when the rain is lashing down outside and through the winter night the road stretches back to Killeaney, furrowed by storms, strewn with sea-weed and sentinelled by strange monuments. Again, I have been happy just working in the sitting-room, pounding the Remington like mad as I hope to pound out these words on it in that very room.

I divided the year into quarters. The first quarter I spent at home in Donard, among the Wicklow Mountains. The second spent in filming, the third in Aran and the fourth in editing the summer's film footage in London. It did not always fall precisely into quarters and I was often out in the island in the winter, but that was the general scheme.

So in the summer of 1939 I was in Aran. I had been in Donard for the Munich crisis but had felt that it would not come to war just then (my astrologer in the Sunday paper backed me up in this) and I did not feel that war was evitable in 1939 either (and my astrologer concurred).

Plans for a documentary film linking the Irish section of the New York World's Fair with its origins at home had fallen through, very fortunately because the war would have caught me in America, and apart from some writing to do I was at a nicely loose end.

But by the spring of 1939 it looked as if things were becoming serious and I thought about joining the Volunteer Force of the Army (just in case) but I have a slight injury to one foot which makes the wearing of Boots, Army Pattern, most unpleasant. I was in the O.T.C. at school when my foot was operated on and after that I retired into the Signals Section, where we set about looking mysterious and never did any parades. I did not mind parades very much but I did mind parades in Boots, Army Pattern, and so Boots, A.P. called a halt to my ambitions in the Volunteers for the time being and I went off to Aran, putting the Volunteers on the long finger and my trust in the astrologer.

But from 1939 onwards this business came to meet people, this is how it came to me. I am never called in the morning in Aran. I am never, if possible called in the morning anywhere because I simply can't get up unless I have something specific and important to do. This July morning I woke and rolled over on my jangling springs. There was something at the back of my mind, but what was it? My eye fell on the candle beside my bed. The Tempest beside the candle, on my heaped clothes and on the window. Outside was a fine driving mist, the wind would be easterly. But what was doing to-day? Ah, it was steamer-day, the day when the *Dun Aengus* calls from Galway with mails and stores and a few tourists. And there was something more, a soldier – an islander from Ier Kerna, near Killeany, had died in Dublin and they were bringing his body home.

Was the steamer in sight? Sometimes it came directly from Galway and sometimes it came by the other islands so I listened to the muffled voices in the bar and the kitchen and soon realised that the steamer was in, fast at the pier-head of Kilronan across Killeany Bay. I went down to the kitchen for a jug of hot water. Mrs Fitzpatrick, Brian her son, and her grandson of five years were there. Going upstairs again I went to the opposite bedroom and looked across at Kilronan, which I could just see in the mist. The funeral was on its way, only visible as a patch of saffron made by the flying cloaks of the 1st Battalion pipers, then a smudge of green – the firing party and escort – and after that a long black moving smudge of shawled women and dark-clothed men winding along the low shore road. I could not her the pipes, only the damp thudding of the drums. Slowly they moved along, the huge natural floor of the ball-alley, up

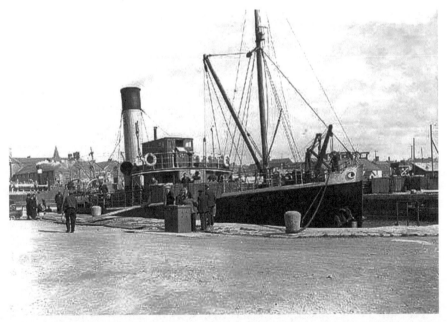

SS *Dun Aengus*, the steamer service from Galway to the Aran Islands.

the hill, past the school-house, past the monuments and past the lowered blinds of our house; then on through the village to the wind-swept churchyard in the sandhills from which the bugle soon sounded waveringly against the breeze. When the funeral was over the escort and band were dismissed and as the crowd passed the house someone called my name. It was Michael Dillane, who eight years before had played the part of the child in *Men of Aran*, I did not recognise him in uniform at first. Then we walked into Kilronan together. Kilronan looked as it always looks on steamer-day, with crowds round the post-office waiting for letters, the stevedore on the quay checking bags of cement from the *Dun Aengus* and tourists taking photographs.

After lunch I went to Mrs. MacDonough's public-house above the harbour and had a drink with Michael and his brother and some soldiers I knew and then the *Dun Aengus* blew and it was time to move. The pipers formed up aft and played a gay air, the soldiers lined the rail, Michael gave me the Irish salute – palm downwards – as the *Dun Aengus* started to move astern, curving round and then going ahead. And suddenly I knew that this was all over for me. It came to me in the sadness of the day, the pipes in the wind, the farewells, the salute – no single clear reason in any one of them but all combining in some way into a portent. This was all the end of something, for me anyhow. I turned away from the emptiness of the pier-head and walked away with the parish priest, listening to the fading music. Would there be a war, I asked him? The officer in charge of the party had lunched with Father Killeen and told him that they were informed in the army that war was certain and – a bit of news for me – that a Marine Service consisting of motor torpedo-boats was to be formed. So, though I was plunged in gloom, I had a clear course ahead of me.

I walked home quickly. Some turf-boats were discharging at Killeeny quay and I could get a letter away in one of them. But whom to write to? I had only one contact with the army, the Officer in Charge of Records in Dublin, so I slipped a sheet of paper into my typewriter and began setting out my modest sea-experience and asking him what was doing. Then I went down to the rutted quay and gave the letter to Cole Mor King as he left for Connemara.

That evening was calm and beautiful, the wind dropped and the house was still. Mrs Fitzpatrick was sitting in the bar, Thomas and his father were down on the quay, mending nets – or something, little Michael was shouting in the distance as he played with the Flaherty children. Brian Fitzpatrick and Michael Lydon, a boy who had come out from Galway to spend part of his school holidays, had gone to a gathering in a house to the westward but I had not felt inclined to go. I felt very sad.

Presently I took some paper and started to work out a radio-script, 'Summer's Death' it was called, and it was based on some lines by Michael Drayton:

> Since there is no help then
> Come let us kiss and part

It was a farewell to all my pleasant life, a farewell to the enjoyment of summer. My theme was that we were all about to undergo a change. The hills and the streams would remain, the sun would set as redly on the western sea, but they would not ever be quite the same for us again. I subtitled it 'A Sentimental Orgy' and very quickly got it scribbled down, to be revised next day. Then I started thinking about the chances of seeing Galway or Cork or Dublin or Belfast in ruins. And England – the familiar places of it – would the Hotel at Restaurant de L'Etoile be spilled into Charlotte Street? How many of my friends would I see again? Would the Chapel of King College, Cambridge, hold empty arms to the sky while the Ramsden Buildings in my own college became a red-brick heap and roaring flames tore from boat-house to boat-house, devouring the shining hulls?

I thought of France. So positively they had told me there that Easter that war was inevitable, that we would not meet again for years. What would become of Camarets, of Arles and Les Baux? What of Vezelay, Auxerre, Sens and Cavalcanti's pretty house – L'Hermitage St. Bond? Who would eat the good food in Duclair and in Rouen, in Paris itself? Was it possible that this thing was actually coming on the world again? In fact, I thought exactly the same thoughts that everyone else was thinking.

By now the little room was rather dark so I got out of my chair, walked into the bar and drank a pint – confidently telling Mrs. Fitzpatrick that there would be no war; no one wants it I said. Then I walked through the warm evening to my visiting house, past the children whispering as they pattered home bare-footed in the dusk. The lamp was not lit and the glow from the fire showed three or four sitting in various parts of the room. A few questions about Europe, comments on the funeral, and then we sat silent with our pipes and cigarettes. Tom O'Brien leaned against the doorway, looking out to sea. '*Ta'n fhairrige ciuin,*' he said, little above a whisper. So it was, a sheet of misty glass stretching over to the dim grey of the mainland. Greatman's Bay and Carraroe, Cashla Bay and Spiddal. Black Head gave its sharp pin-prick from Co. Clare, near us Straw Island answered with its double flash. After the wind and the rain, after the sharpness of news it was an evening of utter calm made deeper by the stirring in the world outside.

I walked home, lit my candle and went up to bed. The bed-springs jangled as they received me once more. I blew out the light and lay looking at the hill-top and the black shape of Temple Benan, that strange oratory. So there was going to be a war after all.

But next morning I didn't believe a word of it. It's not that I rise every day and face the sun in splendor after an invigorating cold bath. Not a bit of it; I crawl out and begin a process of gradually becoming a little less disagreeable through the next twelve hours. But, after all, the astrologer hadn't let me down over Munich and he had been pretty right about some other things since then and 'of course, no one really wants a war' and the sun was shining again.

After breakfast I read through my script, made a few alterations here and there and liked it. Radio Eireann gave a competent production of it two months later. There would be no war, but I found myself going all over the island and wondering when I would see these places again: away to the west as far as I could go, up to Dun Aengus, up to the Black Fort, fishing in Jonny Kenny's boat. There would be no war, but I found myself stopping work as I typed my script and brooding – miles away. There would be no war, but Daly's was loud with old men talking about the Maginot Line as informedly as though they had built it – as Liam O'Flaherty was to remark to me later.

I got a reply to my letter. The Marine Service was only in the elementary stages of organisation on paper and my services would he more immediately useful in the Coast Watching Service, a branch of the Marine Service from which I could be transferred into the Service proper when the time came. O.K. Away went another letter, to the O/C Marine and Coast-Watching Service this time. I set a term to my stay in the island as it seemed best to get in on the ground-floor of this service (though of course there would be no war). But the reply to my letter did not find me in Aran and the war came just before the time I had allotted myself was up. More correctly I should say that the brief preliminaries to war found me still in Aran.

Those last days were amazingly happy. The weather was perfect and it seemed as though I was living through a synthesis of all I liked most in the island. When it did come the first movement of the war caught me in bed. I heard voices in the bar and the kitchen, then faint 'wheeps' of the radio being tuned in. Last night's late news had been unmistakable, now – Stuart Hibbert's voice – that was enough; I did not need to strain my ears for the word Poland. Hitler's patience had finally gone. Now I had to get up. Two clear days before the steamer would come.

They gave a dance in a house in the village and a barrel of stout was rolled to it from Kilronan, lurching from side to side along the dark road and showering brown foam in all directions when it was tapped by candle-light in an outhouse. Now the good-byes became alarming. This business had come to me, good-byes were being said to me and I might never see the island again or, at best, it would only be for very short periods. Even now my life did not seem quite my own.

Packing took up the next day. I always leave the island with far more than I bring to it. A case had to be made for a model of a trawler, books were put in a small crate, suitcases would not close. I remember travelling in France one year with my mother, my grandmother and my brother and sister. We tried the experience of 'travelling light' and it required a small railway omnibus to take us to the Gare du Nord. I can't help gathering objects round me and if at the moment, I had to leave my ship I should require two suitcases, one ruc-sac, one small trunk, a large kit bag and a small kit bag; and with all that would go the Remington, an HMV portable, a gun case and, of course, sea boots, steel helmet and respirator.

The actual leaving of the island seemed swift and that is as these things should be. Handshakes on the quay at one moment and next moment passing the lighthouse with the islands dropping astern as the *Dun Aengus* pounded up the calm stretch of Galway Bay. Army reservists proceeding to their mobilization centre were singing.

As it was Saturday night I could not get a train to Dublin until Monday. I went into a shop next morning and asked for the Sunday papers; among other matters I was curious to see how the astrologer would explain the situation. There were no papers.

'Aren't you aware that there's a European war on?'

'I don't see how that affects the Manchester editions. There's no fighting in England.' I began to get angry.

'Well, God help some people's intelligence,' said the shop-keeper glaring at me, a decent man with whom I had often dealt. Perhaps his comment was right, anyhow that's how the outbreak of hostilities was taking people, and at the time the Irish Sea was supposed to be packed with German submarines and English destroyers. The papers were an hour late and I don't remember what the astrologer's comment on things was, I dismissed him. In ancient days he would not have got off so lightly.

That night I walked out to Salthill with Sam Maguire the County Librarian. He cheerfully told me that my foot would bar me from serving, when I told him about it, and I was rather cross with him. In Salthill we met the captain of the *Dun Aengus* who had been in the Canadian Air Force in the last war and said that he would fly again if they would let him. They didn't but he went to sea and the last I heard of him was that he was serving in a destroyer in the waters round Iceland.

I was off next morning. Just before the train moved there was a sudden buzz of news about the platform. The *Athenia*.

2

Proceeded

At Athlone station I saw steel-helmeted soldiers guarding trucks in a siding. So there it was. Our neutrality had been announced long ago, I believed that it was the right course then and I am convinced that it was the right course now. But neutrality does not connote a country wide-open and undefended and here was my first sight of the country moving to its defence posts.

We ran into Westland Row Station and there I saw a packed troop-train. I don't know where it was bound for but already I was beginning to feel slightly separated from civilians, looking slightly down on them. How often, how often, how often was I to envy them – and in a short time, too.

I collected my car, stowed my baggage in it, Lunched. George, in the Buttery, told me that every variety of press-man was in Dublin. They were making their way to Galway to meet the *Athenia* survivors.

And now for the Marine & Coast Watching Service. As I had not had time to get a reply to my letter I did not know where I should report to and as first sources seemed best I was soon in the presence of the Officer In Charge of Records. That was the last time for a long time that I was able to see an officer right away by simply

Troops guarding the railway.

asking for him. Soon I would begin to come up against Orderly Room strategy and to make circuitous advances.

Yes, Major Saurin remembered all about it. He telephoned while I studied a pencilled caricature of him on his blotter. Go to Portobello Barracks, such and such a Block. Ask for a Captain Heuston, Good afternoon. Good afternoon, sir.

I drove across Dublin to Portobello and went in a civilian, a free man, a tax-payer. Just a murmured 'Captain Heuston' to the P.A. (Military Policeman) at the gate and I was admitted; polite directions and a 'Sir,' no control over me yet. I could still go back. But he knew what I was, recruits were coming in every minute.

I entered Block whatever-it-was and I still remember the sounds of tele-phones, typewriters, door slamming and a voice in the distance shouting, 'That man is to be recruited at once!' Captain Heuston was just dashing out. I was 'that man' – though I didn't know it.

But I wasn't recruited at once. A sergeant asked me to sit down. I sat down, on a kit box it was, and the sergeant continued the writing I had interrupted. He wrote and wrote, only stopping to light a cigarette and have a little chat with me. What on earth could he be writing about? Not about me certainly, nor had the phone messages he received anything to do with me. We sat, and he wrote.

Since then it has often struck me that a seaman looking at me writing must wonder what I am writing about just as much as I wondered what the sergeant was writing about.

This morning in a comfortable Galway hotel, breakfast served by a waiter, a swift and cushioned railway journey to Dublin, a club-sandwich for lunch in the Buttery with an ice-cold drink. Now I am squatting on a hard green kit-box and for all I know an invader may be approaching our shores at this very moment.

'Aren't we England's back-door?' a man had said in the train. 'She must occupy us.'

'We're England's front line, Germany must try to occupy us too,' said another.

At four-thirty the sergeant and I agreed to call it a day. No Captain Heuston. Ten O'clock to-morrow would be a good time to report, said the sergeant. The P.A. let me out at the Main Gate and I was still free.

I went home to my mother's house and started explaining things but I think my intended future had been anticipated and so all that remained for the moment was to consider how much of my gear I should bring to Donard next day and how much I should need in my new existence. A grave mistake – one should enter a service almost naked. The more one has the more there is to cart around. The best soldiers I know keep their civilian suits outside Barracks (maybe in the Mont de Pieté) and their few non-military possessions are kept in a small case; a few photographs, writing materials, prayer-book, rosary and, very often, a history book which is used to settle arguments.

Next day I was back on the green box, but now I was sharing it with another would-be recruit and the sergeant had been replaced by a small red-haired private. He took my particulars. At all stages in my life in the Service my particulars have been taken again as though in a new posting or occupation I became a new man. They formed a considerable bundle and were lost in 1942 and had to be reconstructed.

Name? Christian name … no, not Maurice … Norris – N for, what on earth for? I shyly gave intimate details of my education and explained that the sixth form was not the bottom of the school. Yes, documentary film-director. The boy looked extremely contemptuous and passed on to my companion and then our papers went away. My timid efforts at explaining that I wished to join the Coast Watching as a step to the Marine Service was coldly ignored. From now until about twelve o'clock corporals kept bursting in and trying to recruit me for the infantry. No. I clung to the box and said my little say. I appealed to the boy, hadn't I said Coast Watching? He did not look up. My companion on the box was soon hauled off and later I saw two brothers in the late forties come in to stop their father joining up. Then the sergeant came back, an old friend.

Now. Yes, subject to this and that I would do for the Coast Watching Service. I was to report on nine o'clock next day for this and that. It was all very well, but I had originally only come to the Barracks for information about the Coast Watching Service. Then, maybe after a week – affairs in order –

'I was told to see Captain Heuston …' I began.

'Captain Heuston has gone out.'

'I wanted to find out whether …'

'You'll probably be sent to Wicklow Head.'

So I drove down to Wicklow to look for lodgings as there was no military post there and the coast watchers were all local men, as was the case everywhere.

Lodgings were hard to find, it was only early autumn. The house that finally agreed to take me had no bathroom but, said the landlady, 'You have the river in front and the sea behind.' Nice in January. I closed with them tentatively and drove over the mountains to Donard, where I had to start explaining everything all over again. I was becoming fluent now. Yes, I'm back (I obviously was) but I'll have to be off again at eight o'clock to-morrow. I might be back for week-ends, or on leave, I supposed. I almost rattled the story out to the dogs.

Now came the last great unpacking followed immediately by the first packing. This belt might be useful – and here was a button-stick, of all appropriate things. Oh, and that box of note-paper and I must have some typing paper. And a Shakespeare and what about binoculars? So the collection mounted.

I arrived at Portobello Barracks promptly at nine, a promptness typical of an almost-service man like myself. But this time, for some reason, I left the car in a garage and took the tram to the Barracks. I went into the office like an old hand and about to sit down on the box when I realised that a completely different staff was in the room. Oh, no, another Block entirely now. I found the Block, found the office and said my piece.

'Go over to that sergeant, there.' This sergeant was within earshot and I felt certain he must have heard me the first time. But apparently he had not; I had to say my piece again. Coast Watching, Marine Service, Officer In Charge of Records, particulars of Coast Watching, Captain Heuston …

'… gone out this minute.'

'When will he be back?' I began to stand up for myself.

'Probably not until late to-night.'

'I'll come back tomorrow.'

'Ah, wait a minute.' Shuffle through wire basket.

'David, isn't it? He says you're to be recruited at once.'

I gave it up. I was in the grip of something: utterly bigger than myself.

'Name?'

'Davidson.'

'Christian name?'

'James, Norris – not Maurice – Norris – N for nothing,' and so on to the end.

'Just wait a second …'

I looked for a kit-box but there was nothing. I read all the notices. I looked to all the soldiers writing; The sergeant (my old sergeant under whom I had served for the last few days) came in with the red-headed private. They just looked through me. After an hour I took some slight support from a window. After two hours six of us were waiting. A corporal came in, took up our papers, muttered with the sergeant and said come along. We were off. Round the square, up here, turn there. Through this way, so on and so on to the Medical Hut.

'Name?' I could only suppose that they were trying to break my spirit. One facial twitch, one hysterical cry, and I was unfit for Coast Watching.

'Davidson' – and all the rest of it. After this came the stripping, the weights and measures, the 99s the eyes – the feet. An interested examination. All right, a few questions about fits and lunacy. Dress up. Oh, just a moment – take off your right shoe and sock again. A medical commandant is summoned. He examines my foot. Oh, Sam Maguire, are you going to be right after all? Yet, supposing they do reject me, maybe I can resume a measure of my civilian life? After all, I have done The Right Thing. They might even give me a little badge to show that I had Done The Right Thing.

'All right, I suppose, it's only for Coast Watching.'

No little badge. No more civilian life. I was hustled into another office and an officer hustled a Testament into my right hand and I repeated after him, 'I.'

'I.'

'James Norris Goddard Davidson.'

'James Norris Goddard Davidson.'

'Do solemnly swear ...' At the end of the Oath I paused, suddenly fascinated by the thought that if I refused to complete the very last phrase my attestation might not be valid. I might be free even at this stage, 'So help you God,' said the officer impatiently. 'So help me God.' For better or for worse I was in the service of Ireland.

The next stage was the Quartermaster's Store. Not the actual Store, I imagined, but a larger emergency fitting-out department prepared for the rush of recruits, and there were plenty of us there already.

'Name?' It all began again and when I was fully logged my guide left me, telling me to report back to the office.

'Now, me boy,' said the C.Q.M.S. rising. We began with Boots, Black, Army Pattern, size 10. So there I came bang up against it. My foot is all right for walking any distance or for climbing, but not very good for running and certainly not for exercise in Boots, A.P.

'In my school O.T.C. ...' I felt myself preparing a speech and clearing my throat but thought better of it. We went on rapidly to leggings, breeches, tunic – a rather handsome tunic for recruiting purposes but not ideally suited to field exercises – they were soon withdrawn. Then the forage cap, and a lot of fitting and tilting before the right size would sit at the right angle. After that the 'grey back' shirts, socks, formidable vests and 'long-handled pants'.

'I already have ... I mean I always wear ...'

'So do I, son, but you must be in possession of them.'

Then things come in a rush. Brushes, nail, clothes, hair, tooth, shaving, boot; an excellent razor in – oddly enough – spectacle case with the Army crest on it; mug, plate, knife, fork, spoon; a pair of gloves, a cane. I signed for everything.

'Now ...' said the C.Q.M.S. and made a gesture indicating that the moment had come for me to dress up as a soldier.

This was the end, this was really the parting of the ways. Slowly my easy civilian attire came off and I stowed it in the kit-bag on top of the stuff already there. As each garment came off I assumed its equivalent in cold stiff uniform attire. One more recruit had been dressed. The C.Q.M.S. made me walk about, almost trotted me up and down, rushed over to other recruits, came back to me and tugged at my tunic. Then he altered the tilt of my cap to one more extreme and tightened my belt. I would do. Over all he tried a greatcoat, he tried several greatcoats. An officer came over from one group and tried several more and at last they were satisfied that Davidson was complete.

'Good-luck, now,' said the C.Q.M.S. as I staggered away with my two kit-bags. Could this be me, this fantastic creature rolling along with his feet in huge boxes? Could I be passing the gymnasium of Portobello Barracks where, as a nicely mannered child at his prep-school I had been brought with other children to learn the innocent mysteries of 'On the hands, down! On the feet, up!'?

Back to the Office. Don't leave that Kit there, it will be stolen. Don't leave it there, everything will be pinched on you. To hell with it, I put it down somewhere and was told to go into a room and report to an officer. Now was I to salute? I knew the Irish army salute but I had never been taught it officially, therefore, that knowledge did not exist, just as my private Aertex's had not existed for the C.Q.M.S. Under the circumstances I felt that it would be presumptuous to salute, perhaps illegal – like proving a proposition of Euclid by something in a later book. So I didn't salute and the officer looked a little surprised before he remembered my rawness.

'You're to report to your Post at once. By the way, where is your post? Where would you like to go?'

This may seem unusual but the Service was so under-manned at that time that men were needed everywhere.

What a chance!

'What about the … the Aran Islands, sir. Will there be a Post there?'

There was a shocked silence in the room.

'But that's in the *Western* Command,' gasped the officer. I wondered if he imagined that they ran about in sheep-skins in the Western Command, carrying clubs.

'You're a Co. Wicklow man, have a look at that,' he said hastily, pointing to huge map. I looked closely to see where the Posts were. Bray, no. Arklow might be pleasant. The sergeant had mentioned Wicklow Head and I chose the mean.

'Wicklow Head, sir.'

'Wicklow Head – let me see. Yes, we want men there. Right. Get a Rail Warrant from the Corporal outside, or is the 'bus handier?'

'I have a car, sir.'

'Good. Then away with you, Report to Corporal Smith in Wicklow.'

I began to clump away.

'Oh, by the way, your pay will be thirty-five shillings a week, including ration-allowance.'

'Thank you, sir.'

In all the come-age and go-ery I had completely forgotten about pay. It seemed generous. They'd been kind enough to have me – and all the lovely kit, too. Yes, it seemed generous.

Now to get to the car, I was let through the gate without comment. Later I should have had to produce a pass but I walked ignorantly through and the P.A. undoubtedly took me for what I was, a raw recruit – dull boots, dull leggings and yellow buttons on my greatcoat.

Indeed I don't know how I was let out at all in that state. And now my troubles began, mental troubles. How awful I must look, surely all Rathmines Road was staring, surely the youngest soldier I met could sum me up. Clash-bang went my huge Boots, A.P, my leggings creaked, I sweated in my greatcoat this hot autumn day. And how should one carry this confounded cane.

Clash-bang-slither: left-right-left. Up Rathmines Bridge and down again. Everyone was staring. I was certain of it. If I could have sneaked out of Barracks at night for a trial trip, but here – in broad daylight – ! I dashed into a shop and bought boot-polish and brasso. The women smiled at me, jeeringly it seemed then but I realised afterwards that it was just a kindly smile. I faced the mocking street again and ran straight into Harry Kernoff.

'Hullo.'

'Hullo.' No smile. No curious stare.

'Have a drink?'

We went into a bar beside us and Kernoff immediately started telling me a story about some mutual friend. I don't think it entered his head to enquire about my fancy dress. He behaved as if it was usual to meet Davidson round a bout here in uniform at this hour. When I gave my glib explanation, Marine Service ultimately, Coast Watching and just turned freshly out of Barracks, he nodded as though it was pretty well what he had imagined. Maybe he had, too. Anyhow, he completely restored my peace of mind and when I walked into the garage in Harcourt Street the attendants, who were well used to me as a civilian, did not raise an eyebrow. In fact the state of the world worried people far too much to let them be curious about a tall and ungainly soldier with dull boots.

I had little trouble getting back into Barracks with the car, perhaps they regretted letting me out. Anyhow, here I was, safely back with the gates closed behind me and my kit was still intact. I dumped it in and started to drive off when I was loudly hailed and told to stop. So I'm going to do a Recruit's Course first, I thought to myself. Ah, well. Take this sergeant down to Wicklow with you. More kit in the back and I was driving away with Sergeant Jimmy Turner, not up to my shoulder, as smart a soldier as one would wish to see, and District Sergeant of my area.

'We'll go to Bray first, I want to see the post there.'

I proceeded to obey my first lawful order. Or was it lawful, seeing that it was my car? It was a direct order anyhow. We got to Bray, drove down the

Esplanade and stopped when we could go no further. Bray Head towered up immediately in front of us.

'The Post's on top of that. The building half-way up is the Eagle's Nest and the Post can be contacted by phone from there. A whistle brings them down. Come along.'

I looked around for a zig-zagging track or something which would ease the climb but the little sergeant was ahead of me, leaping upwards like goat, and as I was no longer my own man there was nothing for it but to follow him. Almost instantly my leggings began to drive into the backs of my knees and my ankles because they were too long, and my boots began to chafe my feet. Then my cap started falling off and dropping considerable distances down the slope, my heart pounded and I reamed with perspiration.

When we reached the Eagle's Nest (a restaurant on the hillside) I cunningly suggested that we should whistle from there and wait for a man to come down to us in order to see whether this temporary arrangement really did work but the sergeant was away again already and this time the going was much worse. All right, I muttered to myself, let him race away … I've only been in the army for less than an hour and I'm entitled to show some signs of civilian fatigue.

At the top we found a nice road leading down to Bray. We could have driven right up. I had expected something like that, I am always blind to any side of a problem save the hard side though I am utterly unsuited to facing difficulties; and yet they talk about nature's compensations.

At the top we found a bell-tent, a Coast Watcher in civvies (very few of them were dressed at this stage) and a very tired and unshaven corporal; tired and unshaven because he had not been able to leave the Post since it was put up a few days previously. This was Corporal O'Neill the Wexford footballer, about whom there will be more later on. Both Turner and O'Neill were Volunteers of experience. O'Neill could make the long columns come alive for you as he described the bringing of the guns from the Glen of Imaal to Dublin before the artillery was completely mechanised. Turner's talk was of army bicycles and motor bicycles, girls and Lewis guns. O'Neill was a journalist and a poet, Turner drove a steam-roller and could make even this ugly thing interesting. Both had the gift of vivid description and both were the greatest friends I had during my time with the Coast Watchers.

Suddenly a Commandant and a Captain arrived, they had climbed up by an even harder route, I was glad to see. The officers and N.C.O.s went into a huddle and I withdrew a little with the other private and agreed that things would shake down after a little, maybe.

It was extremely hot and a thin drizzle blew in from seaward. This drizzle, mostly intensified to actual downpour, seemed to be a permanent feature of

Coast Watching, looking back on it. There was another permanent feature of every Post we visited; a Coast Watcher surprised by us in the very act of looking out to sea through the telescope – never suspected that the District Officer or District Sergeant was creeping up on him – duty first, last and all the time; eyes only for the job, a very remarkable sight.

The private and I ran through our small-talk rapidly. We had no shop to talk because our shop was barely open. My boots and leggings were giving me hell and so were the laces of my breeches *and* I was getting very damp and wanted to sit down under the heather but did not dare to do so in the presence of the officers.

Some civilians appeared out of the mist assuming the facetious expression of civilians approaching military establishments of any kind in a sight-seeing spirit. I wiped the expression off their faces by means of a hideous glare and they turned away uncertainly. Anyhow they could tell their families that they knew where at least one of the A-A batteries was – they'd even seen the soldiers.

At last the conference broke up and we struggled down the hill, leaving Corporal O'Neill up there in the rain with his man. An army car was parked beside mine. Sergeant Turner was given volumes of orders, all of which he assimilated unconcernedly and repeated back correctly and without apparent effort.

'Sergeant,' said I, as I turned the car into Newtownmount-Kennedy, 'what about a drink?'

'Just what I was going to say myself,' said Sergeant Turner, indicating the spot. I had made that request after much hesitation, a sergeant is a sergeant and I was only a few-hours private, or Volunteer, rather. It all seemed very encouraging and it made me think that some plans I had in regard to my boots might be workable. And surely this was the moment for taking stock of the position and getting few explanations.

'Sergeant,' I began, 'what will we be doing on this Coast Watching?'

'Watching the coast for something, I suppose.'

'Yes, but ...'

'I know no more about it than you do. I've got yards of orders but won't know what they mean until we get to Wicklow.' He swallowed reflectively. 'I left home this morning to join my Unit and here I am on my way back as a District Sergeant of Coast Watchers.'

What's the use, I thought. I've been practically shanghai-ed into Service, I'm drawing nearer to my job every minute and I don't know a thing more about it. I later found that this was a feature of army life, nothing is divulged until the last minute. On Monday you are told unofficially that you are going to X on Monday week. Nothing happens until Monday week, there is no further news. Then someone suddenly shouts, 'You! Don't you know you're going to X at eleven o'clock.'

Then follows a mad hour and you sit on your kit for the rest of the day, proceeding to X on Tuesday, or Tuesday week or never. Back of it all there is a Reason but it never turns up until afterwards, if it turns up at all.

As we drove on I found it necessary to concentrate when shifting my enormous right boot from the accelerator to the brake pedal without jamming it somewhere. In Wicklow I dropped my conspicuously new kit at my lodgings and drove on to the Guards barracks. Here met a Lieutenant O'Sullivan who asked me who I was and I got out of the car to explain myself. Here's where I work off my first salute, I thought, and smashed my knuckles against the metal hood-support as my hand flew to my cap. Mad with pain I ground out the old, old story – Marine Service via Coast Watching etc.

Lieutenant O'Sullivan was the Acting District Officer … 'Acting' because he was proceeding on duty to Mullingar Barracks and was handing over to a Lieutenant Clarke who was not present. This meant that Turner had to repeat all the orders he had received at Bray, then add Lieutenant O'Sullivan's instructions and keep them all in mind to add to Lieutenant Clarke's instructions. All this was done in the Day Room of the Barracks, our Orderly Room for some time, while I went from one foot to another. Then Corporal Smith, the Post corporal, arrived from Wicklow Head. He was an elderly man with a merry eye, a Post Office linesman in civilian life and he had served in the Signals in the last war. Now he was called up in the Volunteers. Corporal Smith's arrival meant that everything had to be gone through again. The Civic Guard sergeant looked at us patiently, I am sure he was contrasting us with his own smoothly running Force but he didn't know that he was watching the birth of a new service, that Lieutenant O'Sullivan was accoucheur, that Smith and Turner were midwives-in-waiting and that even I had a function – filling kettles for the event, or something.

It all came to this. There would be three Watches, Midnight to 08.00 hrs, 08.00 to 16.00 hrs and 16.00 hrs to 23.59 hrs. Two men would each do an eight-hour watch together, the Post corporal would be present at each change of watch and the District Sergeant would visit every post (5) in his District daily on a push-bicycle (about 60 miles). These were some of the birth pangs.

I went to bed early and was called out of it at about 2 A.M. as a dance-hall near-by was in flames and one of my landladies thought that it might concern my job in some way. I looked at the dance-hall with huge disfavour.

★ ★ ★

Next morning the sergeant and I drove off to report to Lieutenant Clarke, who lived outside the town. Once more the explanations were run through and the three of us drove to the Guards barracks so that Lieutenant Clarke might telephone Dublin. By now my feet and ankles were in the state of soreness which usually came to them on the second day of Winter Sports. The first few paces of each movement were agony and frequently I had to stop and stare into a shop window while I wriggled my toes and tried to ease my feet inside their armour. I spent most of the day sitting in the car, waiting for something to happen and listening to the war news on the car-radio.

Eventually we moved off on an inspection of Posts. At each Post a short explanation of the Duties as arranged at present was handed out and a check was made on the telephone arrangements.

Dalkey and Wicklow Head seemed to be the best off for accommodation. We had a good corrugated iron hut on a cement Foundation. It was lined with wood and had two bunks made of canvas. Near it was the base of a flag-staff and there was a smashed semaphore at the edge of the cliff. A ladder led down from the bare hill-top on which the hut was perched to a steep track which connected with the road across the fields. There were three lighthouses, one was a very handsome and useless structure standing about a quarter of a mile inland. It had been abandoned probably in the early part of the last century. The second was below our hill, on the landward side. It was too high to be of use in fog and was too far inland as well. Much of its arc had been blocked by the land. It had been abandoned and was used as a hostel by the enterprising organisers of An Oige. Women slept in the keepers' old dwellings, men in the tower; I always felt that there was something interesting about that. The third,

Wicklow Head. The Lookout Post is near the buildings on the very top, the other buildings are the An Oige hostel as described. Also note the 'Eire' sign near the rear tower.

and only successful light, was immediately below us, to seaward, and was built, I imagine, very soon after the second. I was never able to get reliable local information about these three lights. The beginning and end of everything seemed to be that the first tower was five-hundred years old, which it certainly is not; late 18th century at the earliest I would say myself.

On a good day we could see the Mourne mountains, Wales, and as far south as Cahore point. The trouble was it wasn't often a good day. The telephone was another trouble. It was in the lighthouse and the climb down on a dark night was no joke. The sixth westerly meridian of longitude ran slap through our hut but caused us no inconvenience.

Somehow or other the Post was manned and every now and then a man was taken away to Dublin to be 'dressed'. With two exceptions our personnel was made up of ex-soldiers who had done their time in the army.

The exceptions were myself and a man called Goodman who had a heavy Old Bill moustache and was known as 'Talla' – I'm not sure of the spelling. This giving of nick-names is a feature of the east coast, on our Post we had 'Talla' 'Derlett' and 'Tommybar' – all inexplicable to me. The others were plain Jacks and Joes.

I began to wonder when my turn for duty would come but the daily round of the Posts continued. One evening in the Sluagh Hall while recruits were being medically examined I found a heap of equipment among which was a pair of nicely softened leggings, I quickly changed mine for an old pair and was much more comfortable. Next day I bought a pair of civilian boots and felt better still.

Then the time came when all the Posts seemed to be more or less organised and we turned our attention to the Duty Roster. I say 'we' because I was becoming quite daring by then and actually made suggestions. One evening, driving the car through the fields and through the seven gates which had to be opened and closed before reaching the Head, we stopped the car, got out paper, and Lieutenant Clarke, Sergeant Turner, Corporal Smith and I worked out a system by which each man got a break of 32 hours in his weekly rotation of eight hours on and sixteen hours off. In our system we split into pairs so that each pair got used to each other's ways. Otherwise it might happen that two men not on terms might come on watch together; in fact it did happen more than once, in spite of precautions, and a very dreary eight hours it must have been. Very sensibly, each Post was allowed to arrange things to suit local conditions, provided that the eight-hour watches were maintained, and our Post ran as smoothly as any.

3

Watches Set

I did my first watch with Corporal Smith one Sunday, quite a bit after I had come to Wicklow. It was only for a few hours in order to simplify our change over to the new routine. Next night I came on duty for a full watch with Volunteer O'Sullivan, a six-foot farmer whose family came from Co. Kerry. Midnight, and Coast Watching, had really started for me.

Eight hours, I said to myself, eight solid hours. I began to think about all that could be done in eight hours. One might have gone from Holyhead to London and a bit of the way back and still we would be on top of Wicklow Head. Some other measure of time now – but I got little encouragement from Tom O'Sullivan for he had been harvesting all day. He sat down on a bunk in the hut and soon fell asleep. I identified all the lights, looked about for coast-wise traffic, looked inland for mysterious signals, saw nothing, yawned and started to pace up and down the concrete path. Eight hours. So this was it at last. Roll on, the Marine Service.

I stuck it as long as I could, looked enviously at the other bunk and compromised by sitting down on the step. Soon I was taking short sleeps, leaning against the door. It was an impossible situation and later the rule became one hour in, one hour out. Coast Watching had really started. The Volunteers were all in uniform, army uniform, though we were the Marine and Coast Watching Service. Our Posts had their first equipment and we logged everything in sight on sea or land. Many were the odd reports telephoned in from the Look-Out Posts to the Intelligence Officers; 'It might be a battleship, sir, or a Submarine' was one. The classic Log Book entry was '*dutch forner camelflug*', which referred to a camouflaged foreign ship of Dutch nationality. Sometimes we were sent reports by civilians. Most of them were made in all sincerity but some turned out to be fantastic. Such a one was the submarine scare.

I was on duty on the 8 to 4 during a thunderstorm when we suddenly saw one of our own aircraft come out of the clouds and proceed to quarter the sea beneath us at a very low altitude. At the same time the telephone rang and, with a tremendous punctuation of static from the lightning flashing round the Head, we were instructed to indicate to the aircraft where the submarine was.

'What submarine, sir?' We were then told that a submarine had been reported to the Guards in Wicklow who had forwarded the information. It had surfaced and immediately submerged again. We could do nothing but assure the I.O. that we had not seen any submarine. But we did plenty when we came off watch. We took a chart and tried to find the originator of the story, but he was missing. We did, however, find two witnesses of 'something in the water'. One gave us a bearing seaward, the corner of a building in line with the pier-head, or something like that. The second witness, an old man fishing on a sort of breakwater, gave us a straight line out to sea. Thus we got a rough fix and the spot was one not visible from our L.O.P. so we could not have been expected to see it. Good. Now, the depth of water at the time. Not nearly enough. Good again. And then the old man casually told us that he didn't know why we were making such a fuss about 'a thunderbolt or something like it' which was what he had seen. Best of all. I never succeeded in contacting the originator of that story, anyhow he overdid it when he described to the Guards the 'railings' and the 'aerials' on a submarine which momentarily surfaced and dived again.

Where we were to blame was in the affair of the trawler, the M—— C——. This business of initials reminds me of the old-fashioned 'Dr. I. K——, a respected practitioner of the town of W——'. I suppose I could mention the trawler's name but maybe it would not do. This also occurred in the 8 to 4 watch. Towards the end of the watch we observed a trawler with her trawl out coming through the banks. She eventually passed right beneath us but had hauled her trawl by then. We had no particular instructions about reporting breaches of the Fisheries Protection Act and anyhow we could not have fixed her position so we just put her in the log. We noticed her trawl on deck and we also noticed that the ship was smart and new, nothing unusual in the C—— Line, and that her name was, as you have probably guessed, the M—— C——.

She anchored on Wicklow Roads and we left word with our reliefs to keep an eye open for any boats going in from her and then we went home. At that time, and for most of the time, my mate was Matt Patchell, a man who had served his time in the army, joined the Volunteers and was now on service again in the M & C.W.S. Neither of us liked that trawl. It was unusual to trawl where she had been, the whole thing looked as if it had been done for the benefit of observers and we were both suspicious.

I had my tea, or lunch, or whatever one calls a large meal at 4.30, and when I calculated that the trawler men would have had time to get squared off and have a meal themselves I set off for the harbour, meeting Patchell. We were right.

The trawler's punt was just pulling in and we met the crew at the steps. Who were they? They gave us name and port. Why were they here? To repair the trawl. So that was the sequence; man trawls, man tears trawl, man has excuse for anchoring and repairing trawl. Had they been trawling, we asked? No. This was bit of a puzzle. There was no doubt that they had been trawling but maybe they thought we held Fishery Warrants and feared being detained here. No, they hadn't been trawling, just out of port in fact, but the trawl *was* torn and while it was being mended they were going to stretch their legs and have a drink. Who was left on board? The Skipper, engineer and a fireman. Mending the trawl? Patchell jumped at that slip. Oh, the trawl was finished. In such a short time?

It was a most improbable story. Patchell went to the public-house with them and I went to the phone and got on to the Intelligence Officer. He told me to go back and find out all I could from them. There were no regulations against trawlermen coming ashore at that time, later an attempt was made to enforce them. So back I went to the public-house. The mate was the man who had done most of the talking but if he was a trawling mate then I was Sir Thomas Beecham, an English naval officer more likely. Some of the others were probably trawlermen, others did not look like any I had met and the new sea-boots and oilskins of all of them appeared to be from the same issue. I made enquiries about trawlers I knew, mentioning another C—— boat, the P—— C——. I also mentioned trawling skippers; and while some of the men were ready enough with their answers, the unlikely men seemed to look to them for guidance, especially the mate. They stuck to the trawl story too and Patchell got no more out of his lot than I did out of mine. I went back to the barracks and called the I.O. again. Were they trawler men, he asked. Some of them certainly were, I told him, the rest did not seem like trawlermen at all. What was their story? I gave it to him. He asked me a few more questions and then told me to tell the men on the Post to keep an eye on the trawler during the night. There was nothing more to be done. Even in those scary days one couldn't arrest a crew for not looking quite *like* a crew.

And here's where I think that crew fooled us. I went back and found the party breaking up. We started to walk down to the harbour and it was very dark outside and the lane was narrow. It became a straggling procession down to the punt and then we said good-night and they pulled off. For some time afterwards Patchell was thoughtful and then he said, 'I think there were fewer going off in that punt than when she came in. Maybe some slipped away in the lane.'

I wasn't sure. The elementary and sensible thing would have been to count the men as they came ashore and as they left but so very often one only thinks of the elementary and sensible thing after the event. We had to leave it like that, we were not sure enough of anything to report anything.

Some days later two Englishmen appeared near Arklow and were reported to the Coast Watchers as having been acting suspiciously. One was identified in Arklow town by the action of a barber who had shaved him and was arrested at Newrath. The other was, I think, arrested in Bray. Posing as tourists they had bought bicycles in Wicklow. Whether they were connected with the M—— C—— I don't know and I don't suppose I ever shall. Trawlermen I spoke to afterwards seemed to know little about the M—— C——. Anyhow, I don't think our first police efforts were very good.

Another episode concerned a mysterious light which, by observation of the turn of the tide, we found to be drifting. What was it? I called my mate again as soon as the light began to improve. It was a wretched dark December morning and we couldn't see anything for a long time. Then it appeared as though the light were on a short mast, but we could see no boat. We got no answer to our morse-lamp. Then something appeared below the mast. A raft? By this time our reliefs had arrived and we all concentrated on it. At last we saw three shapes rolling about below the mast. Three men lying on a raft awash, with a light burning above them? Maybe, but what could we do about it? Wicklow lifeboat was on repairs and we could not on our own responsibility call out a fishing boat. The nearest lifeboat was at Arklow and we hesitated to bring it so far for something we could not even define. To hell with caution, we decided, there was always a chance that it was what it appeared to us to be, and anyhow when the light went out it would become a danger to navigation. We called Arklow, greatly to the annoyance of the Wicklow people we learned afterwards. Then we reported to the I.O., signed the Log, saw the others sign the Post Inventory Book and drove off to breakfast.

In the end a local boat beat the Arklow lifeboat to the object which turned out to be a large dan buoy trailing three bladders. I tried to get the lamp – a very fine one – from the Receiver of Wrecks but I did not succeed.

At this time of year when doing my week on the midnight to eight a.m. watch I never saw daylight. It was dark coming off watch and dark again when I got up in the evening.

Then there was the radio episode. We had a wireless set in our hut, we had hired it and what a bone of contention it turned out to be – each watch accusing the others of using more than their fair share of the batteries. This passing of the buck was a feature of our lives. A and B would come on watch and find the Primus empty. Who used all the oil they ask C and D at the change of watch. The oil? Oh, when we took it over from E and F last week it was always empty. At the end of that watch E and F arrive and C and D ask them the same question. If they are friends with C and D they will say that, 'We gave the bloody thing full to A and B yesterday.' If they are enemies it will be, 'Ask yourselves, you gave it to us empty yesterday.' Eventually the stove was always left empty and the hut was surrounded by private hides of paraffin.

But to return to the radio. One evening during my hour inside the hut I was listening to morse when I picked up an unidentified S.O.S. It was repeated for a long time and I was wondering whether we ought to pass the Call-sign on to the I.O., it was not part of our duties, when Portpatrick Radio came through on telephony and so did the originator of the distress call. It was a Liverpool pilot-boat – of all craft – ashore near, I think, New Brighton. They were calling for a lifeboat and for shipping to stand by and she was full of candidates for Pilot's tickets who were undergoing examination. A passenger ship on the Bar of Liverpool said that she would stand by but could not venture close in. It appeared to be a dirty night over there though it was calm with us. We followed the whole incident. Then the master of a coaster came through on R/T and said that he'd be so-and-so'd if he would stand in for anyone; it was blowing a half-gale and the rain was making it as thick as a bag. Eventually the Pilot boat's operator could be heard talking to the lifeboat. Right up to about 3 a.m., when his signals faded, he was calm and cheerful. It was a bit of a shock to read in the papers some days later that she had been lost with all hands.

The breaking of the telephone wires in sleet storms was another feature of life and it entailed hours of floundering round in waist-high heather attempting to find and meet the ends.

And each Post round the coast had its tales of similar incidents.

As the winter wore on I decided to live in the hotel and leave my lodgings. I wanted a bath in the mornings, or on coming off duty, and 'the river in front and the sea behind' was still the only possibility. Just then I was reading H'siung's 'The Importance of Living' and the book ceased to be quite such a reproach to me after the move.

One evening before this I was sitting in the hotel bar and heard a voice coping with the telephone. The box was in the hall and conversations could be overheard. It was all about a party and the telephonee was being 'sirred' –presumably the father who had stood the racket – and it became clear that there had been a slight racket, almost a little incident, nothing serious at all but the telephoning was just a very nice apology and apparently all was well.

The young men came into the bar and we were soon talking. I explained myself and one of them said that he lived nearby at Rosanne; his name was Corballis and this was his cousin. Somehow or other it turned out that his father had been at the same college at Oxford as my brother was afterwards at, and then things just flowed along. I was invited to lunch next day, to many lunches, eventually there was a standing invitation to any meal. Bless that family, they kept my spirits up. When I thought that there never would be a Marine Service and that I would be stuck on Wicklow Head for ever I used to reflect that after all there would always be the Corballises not so far outside the town.

The house was late Queen Anne or early Georgian – mellow brick and stone – with a private chapel and a ghost I never quite believed in, one of the houses which feel warming and welcoming the moment one enters them. It had a sort of Dingley Dell combined with Sir Roger de Coverly atmosphere of welcome. It seemed as if something was always just about to happen or had just happened – but most frequently something was happening at the moment one arrived; anything from a Hallow'een party to a dance in the house or in an hotel, such as one at Greystones where the proprietors thought my uniform was fancy dress and objected to my boots, most difficult. How those boots did follow me around.

There was Captain Corballis, Mrs Corballis, her mother, a daughter and two sons of which the elder was Jerningham – whom I had met in the hotel. 'That's a hell of a name for you, wha'!' a Wicklow man said to me. 'They got that out of the Greek bible for him.' I always liked to picture the Corballis parents sitting with a Greek testament between them and running their fingers along the lines until they come to Jerningham and then saying 'Ah, the very thing!' There was usually a sprinkling of aunts, cousins and other ranks in the house too. What fun those evenings were. One even proceeded to the L.O.P. at midnight in a better frame of mind after leaving Rosanna and it made the 08.00 to 16.00 watch pass more quickly if I was going on there after coming off watch.

But apart from this it was a period of solid discomfort made up of odd little chunks of experience. One of these was pay day. After some months we were paid by cheque on the L.O.P. with all the ritual of a pay-day except that the Corporal handed out the cheques. Before that all of us except the men on watch were paid in the Guards Barracks. I remember one pay-day when we were lined up in the hall of the Barracks waiting for the District Officer. There were footsteps outside, the corporal brought us to attention, we looked to our fronts and were considerably startled when we heard a harsh voice shouting, '... A fine body of men, God bless you, but oul' Hittler's Coming for you – mark my words.' This came from one of Wicklow's characters, a gaunt elderly lady with a superb carriage who promenaded the streets with ready comments on everything and everybody she saw.

'Keep away from him, he's a married man,' she once warned a little girl of ten in my presence. This lady was entering the Barracks to interview her favourite Guard about some grievance. She had many, but about once a year she would air one to such purpose that the Government would become aggrieved itself and remove her elsewhere for a spell.

When we were paid by cheque on the L.O.P. we usually followed this by cashing the cheques in Mr Byrne's house opposite the Memorial and sometimes these functions would last until closing-time. Then 'Talla' Goodman would sing to us and then my mate, Matt Patchell would recite from the Vickers Gun manual. Those gatherings had the queer mad gaiety of the prisoners before Christmas in Dostoevsky's *Letters from the House of the Dead* [sic]. You remember how they were led to the steam house and as they laid about them with twigs to open their pores, raised above their wretched selves on this one day of all the year, they sang a song called Kamarinskaya .

So time crawled on; out on the forenoon watch, scrambling up to the Post through the darkness to relieve the night men and watching the day come; down again at four in the afternoon. Or up in the fading afternoon light and on until midnight, the best watch. Or fighting off sleep while waiting to go on watch at midnight. Hour in, hour out: day in, day out. And the same thing all round the coast.

I often thought of the other man on the next Post, and the post after that, right round from Donegal to Ballagan Point. Sometimes we telephoned Kilmichael or Bray about something seen north or south of our post, with a grumble about the weather and conditions in general thrown in. A watch seldom went by without something being reported. There is no doubt about it that this Service should have been maintained after the war, instead of that its trained personnel were scattered. The original coastguards were not there for nothing and the purely civil uses of the Service were countless. For the fisherman in distress, for the pilot expecting an overdue ship, for those involved in a cliff-climbing accident – the Coast Watchers were at the service of all those, and they proved their worth. Reduce the personnel and turn the Posts into dwelling-houses by enlarging them and our coasts could be permanently watched without the weary journey out to the post which caused such hardship during the Emergency. Add to them the Coast Life-Saving Service, and the Light-house Service and the Lifeboats, make them into a whole controlled by the Marine Service and what have you? – something impossible or a simplified organisation of four essential services?

All the time I kept the Marine Service to-be in my mind, bothering the District Officer to know if he had heard anything yet. And when I settled down to Coast Watching much as I ever did I began to think of preparing myself as far as possible for the Service. My seamanship was sufficient for myself in my own boat and, under guidance, it served in fishing-boats of various kinds but it went no further. My standard of navigation was about as high; very good in fair weather but quite untried in any emergency, though I did bring a boat from Baltimore to Valentia through dense fog, laying off my courses on an old blue-back chart with a bicycle pump for a parallel-ruler. Soon I was to learn that the prudent master would not have left Baltimore. A correspondence course seemed to be the best way of acquiring more knowledge and soon I had enrolled myself with a famous London firm, Captain O.M. Watts Ltd. The whole course arrived together and my lessons began to cross to London through two censors and then to return to Wicklow with red-ink comments varying from the pleasantly encouraging, through the firm, to the downright nasty. Soon the eight-hour watches were flying by with one hour out followed by an hour's work at the test-papers and then another hour out.

I made the acquaintance of Tait's very concise *Guide To the Home Trade*, *Burton's Tables*, the intimidating *Admiralty Manuals of Navigation*, *Reed's Seamanship*, *Tait's Seamanship*, *Clissold's Seamanship* (later a portion of the kit of every Seaman in the Service) and two books by C.H. Brown which I still read for pleasure and instruction, *Meteorology for Masters and Mates* and *Deviation and the Deviascope*, models of what a text-book should be.

I began to work at signals too. I was fairly hot at Morse by ear, lamp or flag but I did not know Semaphore at all so I set out to learn it by a system of my own, i.e., learning all the letters that could be made with one flag and then regarding the remaining letters combinations of these, F and A making M etc. With the help of Frank Ryan, one of the keepers in the light-house, I was able to speak to him fairly rapidly in two days. Brennan, another volunteer, could semaphore too and soon everybody could, and then I started teaching morse to Patchell, and Jack Kavanagh, another watch-mate.

I heard I. A. Richards say in a lecture on Criticism (in a rough paraphrase) that a determined effort to find and analyse the 'bad' in anything often uncovered an overwhelming amount of good. I have gone back over my Coast Watching time and unearthed these interesting periods of working on Navigation and Seamanship and Signals but they could not overwhelm the 'bad'. Coast Watching was tough and necessary but there was no good in it because it was entirely without compensations. Sometimes on a calm night I would halt on my beat and look over the mountains and think of my comfortable home inland, or look north at the flash of the Bailey Light and think about a warm bed in my mother's house. I would suddenly feel outside myself. 'What on *earth* are you doing here?'

Again, I was just thinking like thousands and thousands all over the world. Doing nothing, ready to do something if anything happened. This was usually followed by some boy-scouty reflections on Preparedness and then the cold would get me and I would move off again in my boots, creaking leggings and funny cap. The bother of it was that one could not just march up and down thinking of nothing – in fact marching up and down was the wrong thing altogether; the correct procedure was an unwinking examination of a considerable area of sea and hinterland followed by a few short bursts up and down the cliff-top to warm up.

One day engineers appéared and fenced in our hut and the concrete path leading to it, alarmed by a horror-story we had of a coastguard who had been blown away. Then they laid the concrete foundations of a new hut. Much later the builders themselves arrived in a lorry in which they lived and started to set up the concrete blocks and window frames which had been delivered to us. Moving round the country in an anti-clockwise direction these men had built huts all round the coast, gradually cutting their times down. I think our hut went up in forty-eight hours. Possibly forty-nine hours would have made a better job of it. From these men I learned how to make poteen in a kettle but I have never been able to give the method a trial.

As I have said, we were lucky in having a comfortable Admiralty hut already. The new hut had a fine field of vision, large opening windows and a fireplace, but the wind forced the rain through the window-frames, it poured under and around the door, it streamed through the roof and down the walls, and the fire would not draw.

After a week or so of dismal complaints up and down the line, and between ourselves and Dublin, we got to work with putty and tar and fitted an oil-drum round the chimney to make it draw. In the end the hut dried up quite well and by the time I left our only inconvenience was two or three inches of water in the south-easterly corner and duck-boards and rubber boots helped us a lot, though sometimes it was pleasanter outside.

Coast Watch on duty.

Finally, when we could positively identify a part of the wall which was never more than merely clammy, the Post Office/linesman (ex-Corporal Smith, they reclaimed him) removed the telephone from the old hut to the new.

The telephone had a switchboard which connected the light-house below us to the Post Office system on a party-line for the two of us. Every morning the watch going off duty would throw over the switch after we had heard the news by radio and call up Frank Ryan, the assistant-keeper, who would also be digesting the B.B.C.

'Well?' he or we would inevitably say, and the other would come back with his observations on the news. 'Ah,' Ryan would conclude, 'they haven't half started anything yet, they haven't *quarter* started. Wait till they really get going and then you'll see the slaughter.'

In those days of 1939 I never quite believed him, another Sunday paper had taken my fancy. But I was to learn better.

English Sunday papers of the usual thickness could be had on Sundays, as before, but gradually everything began to slow down. Petrol coupons arrived and so did the infamous Black Market. Shortness of articles of luxury food began to be discussed. We turned in on ourselves and theatrical companies began to boom, replacing the English touring shows. Much talent was discovered then which might never have come to the top otherwise. In fact, though the war-time privations were just beginning to be felt, things had never seemed as gay as they did on my visits to Dublin – perhaps by contrast with the bleak Look-Out Post.

And all the time, encouraged by fantastic rumour, we discussed the question of whether we were going to be invaded, and by whom, and how soon we would be ready to put up the best resistance possible. Recruiting went ahead and the formation of the originals of the L.S.F. and L.D.F. began to be discussed. But, of the Marine Service, silence – or more rumours. Indeed, a member of the Civic Guard who said he had positive inside information that there would be no Marine Service urged me so strongly to apply for a transfer into the army proper instead of remaining indefinitely in an unarmed service that I almost did so, for I had no doubt that we would be invaded, maybe in less than a year. Many others believed the same and the general tone of army instructions was never 'if the balloon goes up' but always 'when the balloon goes up'.

And so the winter found us, that terrible freezing and drenching winter of 1939/40 that had no mercy on those condemned to hour in, hour out. Even while the Posts were being established the rain soaked us and then Autumn gave way to the intense cold, the blizzards of sleet, the fogs and the easterly gales.

Having the car, Patchell and I were fortunate to be able to drive, if the weather was not too bad, almost to the foot of the ladder leading up to the post. But often I had to deal single-handed with the seven daemonic gates which barred the road across the fields because I was always a very bad relief and Patchell or Kavanagh or Brennan would walk on ahead of me. The opening and closing of the seven gates in a high wind was not easy. I would prop one open and no sooner was I back in the driving seat, or better still (from the point of the gates) actually driving through, then the wind would swung [sic] them across and bang them against the wings. One night in a fog Patchell and I got off the track and completely lost our bearings, turning the car until he snuffed the damp air and announced, 'We're heading the right way anyhow, I can get the hum of Lacy's dung-heap.' Another night we actually mounted this eminence, steering on the nose and misjudging our distance run.

Patchell was a constant delight, his brown, wrinkled face always carried a grin. The acting of situations was his specialty, especially when it was his turn to be out and the weather was foggy (and if it was foggy we could not see the light-house below us, much less the sea). One fantasy was that the District Officer on a night surprise-inspection was trying to come up the ladder. It was a monologue.

'How am I to know you're the District Officer? – Everyone knows his name, that's no guarantee – Not in uniform either – oh, you can explain and explain but I have me orders. Come up that ladder with your hands up.' The telephone pole would then become the District Officer.

'So you're the District Officer, huh?' and a savage blow with a stick 'No uniform, huh?' Another blow. 'Approaching a military post in the middle of the night with a yarn like that,' then a hail of blows during which an imaginary object would fall to the ground. 'What's this? Identity card and Photograph.' Now he would salute and change his tone. 'Oh, good-night, sir. Foggy night, sir. Thought I recognised you but I wanted to make sure, sir. What! Put me under arrest? I was only doing me duty. Oh, begod now, how do I know this card isn't faked? What kind of a fool do you think I am?' etc etc etc.

He it was who invented the idiotic 'Eire plane' gag. It was brought into one of the many imaginary conversations we used to have with the I.O. – into the microphone all right, but with the rest pressed down. This conversation was supposed to be a report of one of our aircraft having been sighted and I, standing outside, would speak for the I.O.

'What nationality is this aircraft? '

'It's an Eire plane, sir.'

'You've already told me that it's an aeroplane where does it come from?'

'It came from the East, sir, and it's turning South.'

'I don't want to know its course again, I want to know its country.'

'It's an Eire plane, sir.'

'Damn it to hell, man, I know it's an aeroplane! *What Nationality?*'

'An Eire plane, sir.' And so on with the comedy until he got tired. Very simple things, but things which amused us on that bald hill-top.

4

Various Courses

All this time the army was busy on our behalf, we were not forgotten. Though the coming of war had not found the Marine and Coast Watching Service anything like completely organised, the army was not long in setting to work to train instructors and arrange courses. As far as one could make out the best features evolved by the various Posts were eventually collected and embodied in the ultimate organisation. In this sense the Service made itself, and even though rules as to hours, Duty Roster etc. were eventually dictated to us we were told quite clearly that each Post has a separate problem, depending on its situation and where its personnel lived. Consequently, small variations in routine were permitted from Post to Post provided that they conformed to the broad outlines laid down, a very thoughtful, sensible and effective method of administration.

Suddenly the long arm reached out from Dublin and Kavanagh was swept away on a course. He looked like a new man when he returned. Shortly afterwards I was driving across the fields to take up the 16.00 hrs watch, when I saw the track barred by 'Tella' Goodman looking like a prophet of old, arm upraised, fire in his eye end foreboding in his voice.

'You're to go on a Course to-morrow.' That was music to me. To get away from the Look-Out Post, to get near to where the Marine Service must – surely must by now – be stirring in the womb.

'You're to take your full kit with you the message said.'

No bother, no bother at all. I put my clothing bag and my kit bag in the back of the car next day and set off for Dublin.

The course was to be in Collins Barracks, Dublin, so I arranged to garage the car at a near-by hotel and then reported to Portobello, our place of assembly. Most of the Course was already there but there were still some trains and buses to come in. I noticed with alarm that all the rest were corporals. We had only an acting-corporal on our Post. Surely they did not mean to make me a corporal, confirm me, as it were, in the Coast Watching branch instead of the

Collins Barracks, Dublin.

Marine Branch? Pondering over this I waited with the rest. It was like first day at school, only everyone was a new-boy. We waited on both feet and then we shifted the weight from foot to foot. We leaned against the wall, perched on radiators, sat in windows or paced up and down. We waited and waited as I had waited five months ago. The same N.C.O.s with papers rushed by us and still we waited. Then, when I was beginning to get a dim feeling that we were about to be told to go back to our Posts and report again in a fortnight's time there were shouts, 'Come on! Hurry on! Are you going to be there all day?' and eighty of us, with our kits, were packed into lorries and sent whizzing through Dublin to the other side of the river.

Collins Barracks. A handsome grey building. Heavy green doors being opened by the military police and then – slam! There we were. Spinning round corners now, from square to square, until we stopped in Connolly Square. No one liked to be the first to get down. A Company-Sergeant with papers, naturally and an entourage of minor N.C.O.s, came out to look at us with an expression of disfavour.

'Are you the men from the L.O.P.s?' he shouted. One began to wonder indignantly if he thought we were eighty men reporting to the Curragh on a Cooks' Course and delivered here instead – and so we might have been, but my military experience was not great enough for me to know that such a mistake could have been made. Someone admitted for us that we were from the L.O.P.s.

'Have you got the unconsumed portion of your rations with you?' Our spokesman said that we were on Ration Allowance.

'Then you'll get *word*-all for tea.'

I think it is Patrick Campbell who has pointed out that no military operation can ever be successfully undertaken without the use of the word *word*. Certainly I realised that it was a buttress and mainstay of our L.O.P., used – as Campbell said – in a manner defying analysis. I was soon to learn the full range of the uses of this word *word*, its tremendous permutations, combinations, and employment as noun, adjective, adverb, verb and preposition – apart from exclamation. For some reason, in the army generally and certainly in the Marine Service, *word* was to die away to a large extent in a few years. Used so often it lost its power, though in moments of stress the seaman will still let it fly in a form full of feeling if not of intelligible meaning.

We dragged our kits up outside stairs and moved to the quarters assigned to us and I met my first barrack-room, or rather, two rooms with an arched wall between holding two fireplaces backing each other. Buff-coloured distempered walls and wooden beams of the same colour, black iron racks, bare boards and two huge turf fires blazing away. The walls were decorated with reproductions of hoists in the International Code. When I woke on my right side I saw an example of a Bearing Hoist, my left aspect gave me the

A typical army barrack room.

Palindrome Navan – illustrating the use of the Second and First Substitutes. There was a heap of bed-boards, a heap of trestles, a heap of mattresses and a heap of blankets, sheets, pillows and pillow-cases.

We started to construct beds, three planks supported about six inches off the deck by two trestles. We drew our bedding. We sat down to wait for something to happen. New boys – new school – new dormitory, and what a dormitory. Spotlessly clean, oddly decorated with the flag diagrams, but a room that could never have been anything other than a barrack-room from the time of its building. I could imagine regiment after English regiment, stretching back to scarlet coats and pipe-clay, full of the hoping, despairing, praying, believing, grumbling and plenty of *wording* that is carried on to the present day, It was the most grim, inhuman and rigidly disciplined thing that I had ever seen, the diagrams looked like the follies of a great man, the fires his secret vice. Yet I grew very fond of that room, and very proud of it, with its scrubbed floor, rows of bedding, neatly stacked boards, kit-boxes dressed in perfect lines, kit-bags ranged on the racks and our polished sea-boots gleaming in two lines.

In a corner, on a real bed, a young regular corporal was writing. This struck me as being the genuine military thing. His green web, steel helmet and respirator were slung over his bed with meticulous accuracy. His rifle was at the head of his bed and his kit was on the rack above, apparently folded and moulded into one mathematical block. And he was writing, writing home? Yes, this was perfect. The young soldier remembering the old folks. I felt a bit like writing myself.

And then he suddenly sat up, shouting, 'Cut out that talking, now, and pay attention,' and proceeded to call the roll he had been writing from our papers (farewell the old folks). After that there was a slight re-shuffle of beds and we were grouped round the room in the order in which our Posts ran in the Eastern and Curragh Commands. On the other side of the partition was another corporal with the Southern Command, and the Western Command was in a different room.

'Now,' said the corporal, 'I'm going to show you how I want to see your bedding made up in the morning.' He showed us. The first blanket folded lengthways; then alternate layers of blanket and sheet placed with the blue stripe of each sheet exactly at the fold; the tight packing of the layers in one round of the first blanket; the inversion of the whole and the placing of the pillow and greatcoat on top.

'Simple, isn't it?' he said, smiling. We smiled agreement. 'Well, that's the way I want see you *wording* do it *every* morning,'

Next he showed us how to fold our greatcoats so that the belt buttons came out exactly in the middle and I began to realise that though my mates were all corporals most of them had not been long in the army. Then the room itself.

'I'm going to appoint a room-orderly for every day. You – yourself in the bottom corner, Cahore Point, you're first. And I want to be able to see my face in the floor. The room orderly will stay in here all day except when he's relieved for meals and he'll be responsible for the tidiness and cleanliness of the room. He'll draw turf for the fire with the other room-orderlies but he won't light it before 16.30 hours. And do you see this grate?' We saw it. 'If I don't see these bars shining every morning then I'll make you polish them with your *wording* tooth-brushes and brush your teeth after that. O.K.?' And from the adjoining room I heard the other corporal talking about toothbrushes.

'O.K., then. Make down your beds.'

During the bed-making he brought us up one by one to explain our personal attainments. Yes, it was name, rank, number, home address – all the rest of it again. Military experience? We stumbled over O.T.C. because he thought I meant the army O.T.C. Foot-drill? Yes, I remembered most of it. Signals? All right in all branches I boldly said. How about morse? Yes, morse above all.

'Good,' said the corporal, 'I want to work up my morse.' Next man, yourself, Howth Head.

As the C.S. had promised us, we got *word* all for tea, but we were told that our names were on the Pass-Roll at the gate and that we were free until ten o'clock. So I set off through the Square and on to the foggy Esplanade which led to the Main Gate. I saw a vague figure in the distance and heard him shout something like 'Evening'.

'Good evening!' I came back readily.

'Evening!' shouted my friend again, or so it seemed.

Kit and bedding correctly made up. Note the three buttons at the back of the folded greatcoat facing out!

'Good-evening.'

'Evening!' and other words followed accompanied by the rattle of a rifle-bolt coming back and going forward. Thus I met my first flying-sentry and learned to keep my ears open for their commands.

'Have you got a pass for those?' The P.A. at the gate pointed at my civilian footwear which I had forgotten about. Oh, God, was it going to be boots again?

'I can't wear army boots, corporal.'

'I can't help that, you must have a pass.' Muttering, I walked back to our quarters and spoke to the corporal there. 'See the C.S. about a Pass.' I saw the C.S. about a pass.

'Do you think I'm going to walk round the *wording* Barracks at this hour getting passes signed? Go sick in the morning.'

Go sick, the indispensable prelude to anything concerning the body. Meanwhile I decided to wear the Boots, A.P. for one evening.

'Turn down the collar of your coat,' said the relentless P.A. letting me out.

Though I had been in Dublin in uniform several times I had not worn army boots in Dublin since September saw me clashing down Rathmines Road. I looked for the car. Garage locked. Man with key gone away. So there I was. Oh, maybe a very fine and efficient figure on the Look Out Post, able to reel off bearings, depths, distances, types of craft and all that we were required to know – it wasn't much – but in Dublin a plaything of the military machine, and a plaything in iron-clad boots. I got something to eat and went back to the Barracks.

My bed was comfortable. I like a fairly hard bed and the boards sagged nicely. Apart from the daily bother of dismantling and re-assembling them they are more comfortable than iron army beds. The best way to make one up is to set the three boards into the shape of a shallow trough. With mattress, sheet and blanket below, and sheet, three blankets and a great-coat on top I found it pretty good. I was sleeping beside the hero O'Neill, the corporal whom I have already described as living on his Post for a fortnight so as to get things running properly.

We settled down sleepily and peacefully to the lawful occupation of cribbing about all things connected with the Service. Then, one wriggle to bring the bedclothes over my ears and I was blinking at the glow of the dying fire, but not for long. There is no need to describe *reveille*. Blown well or ill it is still an infuriating summons. I will pass over, too, the voice of the Orderly-Sergeant, anyhow his calculated insults always drove me more deeply into the blankets, deliberately deferring my rising. Somehow I found myself washed, shaved, breakfasted and paraded to the Medical Hut, where I whipped off my right boot and was hastily prevented from telling all about my operation by the M.O., who scribbled out a Pass vouchsafing permission to 207630 to wear Civilian Boots.

And now our first parade. We fell in and the first word of command came – in Irish. All the Irish I know – and few have had such good opportunities for learning it – could be inscribed on the head of a fairly large pin. Certainly it was not good enough to recognise strange words of command. But I rightly anticipated what the first command would be. Anyhow, it is not on the actual words of a command that one works, it is on the sound. A Sergeant-Major at school used to roar, 'Eeed! Eeed oin! – O-ope ipe!' and the parade would come to attention and slope its arms. Written down for me I might have understood the meaning of the words but coming stridently from Corporal Dolan it was, as Robert Flaherty said of a gesture, 'worn smooth by time'.

'*Paraid! Paraid! – aire!*' It was an easy guess that we would be brought to attention.

'*O deis deasuigid!*' And obviously we would dress by the right.

'*Dearcaid romaib!*' And eventually we would have to look to our fronts. We did very well up to this. Had I been right-hand man I would have been stumped when the command came to number off, but the right-hand man was experienced and the numbers in Irish came rippling down the line, or tottering down the line I should say because it needed several repetitions before we all got it right.

'*Deas iompuigid!*' I stepped back and to the right, expecting a movement the same as forming fours. Then I got back into my place with the rest of the hesitaters.

'*Do reir o deis – go mear mairseail!*' We marched off together for the first time and we looked *wording* awful. But we had begun. For a week I was too busy, and then I borrowed a manual from Paddy O'Neill which gave the words whose sounds were by now so readily obeying.

Some years later I found that English was being used more than Irish in the words of command. I never understood why. On that Course men of as old as fifty-five with no Irish at all had no trouble in picking up the commands, and the sound of the commands in Irish surpasses any that I have heard in any language. For example, can you equal the whip-lash of consonants in, '*Cun cigireacta – teasbeánaid – airm!*' (For inspection, port arms).

Under O'Neill's expert tuition I found out that it was foolish to fall in early and on the right at meal parades. Even though almost everyone on the Course was a corporal we fell in for meals and did not use the Mess.

The cook-sergeant usually used to sally out of the cook-house and call the last two men in to the very mild fatigues of carrying stew some ten yards to the Dining Hall or helping with the vegetables. After than [sic] one had a rich reward in a cook-house helping and I often found this very beneficial at break-fast when we sat down –only slightly after the others – with a heavily laden plate and a mug of strong tea. Others observed this but by then we were well dug into the cook-house and the cook-sergeant regarded us as his own. The only mistake we ever made was with a bucket of tea. The cook-sergeant poured a tin of condensed milk into it and we helpfully seized metal spoons and stirred. There was a roar from the fat man,

'Do you *worders* think you can teach me my *wording* business? Would you like me to hand over me bloody stripes to you – eh!'

Apparently there was an exact moment, or so he said when the lump of condensed milk should be stirred through the tea, not a second sooner or later, and morning after morning he would keep us waiting – peering into the steaming bucket until he would accept a spoon from us and, in all his majesty, stir.

Training on the Square was broken up with lectures, rather confusingly broken up it seemed at first as we were hurried out into the keen air to Form Double File while Retiring after a lecture on Optical Instruments; and the more we worked the keener grew our appetites for food and sleep.

After lunch on our first day I sank down against my rolled-up bedding and started to fill my pipe while trying to keep my eyes open. Oh, blessed forty minutes that still remained to us. Enter Corporal Dolan briskly and with a morse buzzer in his hand.

'Who's the man who says he knows morse? Yourself, Wicklow Head, come up here.' No sleep for me. I sat down on an army bench at a trestle table and he started to send to me, faster and faster. Then I sent to him. I remember what we sent, too. We used to morse out chapters of *The Rains Came*, and in this way we read a lot of the book.

Most of the men were learning semaphore signalling for the first time, others had forgotten it, and a few actually knew it. On the command in Irish 'Party – for the purpose of signalling –' we would spread out to arms' length and start learning our A-B-C.

'The first circle, by the front, begin!' This pastime was carried on in the billets, too, in the evenings after tea – especially towards the end of the army week when last pay-day was a memory only. The student usually began to spell small four-letter words – *word* being a popular one – and then he expanded to sentences. Then we were marched out to the Park, a clumping rubber-booted crowd, to signal over distances, and I managed to work up a fantastic and utterly useless speed (because only we could read it) with Corporal Dolan.

We also did time at Baldonnel Aerodrome, examining aircraft and studying them for recognition purposes; later on they flew over us in the Park.

It was not always quite so pleasant. We were ordered to scrub the billets. I managed to confine my work to carrying water because they told me I wasn't very good. It was a cold winter evening and the water turned to ice on the floor as we worked. Two men went to hospital after that night's entertainment.

Our best and most useful exercises were the field-days when we were brought to the sea-side at Balbriggan or Howth. There we used to set up dummy L.O.P.s, running field-telephones back some hundreds of yards to a field exchange and then on to a table at which sat an officer representing the Intelligence Officer on duty. On our first day we set up our L.O.P. on the sea-shore. Someone remarked that the tide would soon flow up to it.

'No,' said Corporal Dolan, 'because I was here a fortnight ago and it was ebbing then.'

We digested that one.

These exercises were the only times we all worked together. Apart from lectures we were split into sections. After the preliminary wiring-up of the telephones they used to give us an imaginary incident which was supposed to be going on, and each man of each section made a report on it from one of the four L.O.P.s. The officer in charge criticised the collected reports, gave a lecture on the performance in general, and then invited discussion. It was at one of these conferences when wind direction and velocity was being discussed that one man emphasised his point by the quite incredible reason that, 'I know, because that bird is the only bird that can fly backwards.'

Most of the field-days were carried out in bad weather and the journey in the open lorries was so cold that we once had to throw a man's cap overboard for the pleasure of warming ourselves by running for it.

During this time I publicised my intentions regarding the Marine Service so well that I was told one day not to parade, to stand by for an interview at eleven o'clock. I shivered in the billets all day (no fires until evening). No interview. I had not by then realised that things in the army did not always turn out as they were expected to. Next day I had the interview with our second-in-command Captain (now Commandant) O'Connor. I told him the whole story, I was very glib indeed by then; he listened, made notes and promised nothing, but I was greatly cheered and felt that things were moving. The following week-end the famous M.T.B. *M.1* arrived in Dun Laoghaire, first of our motor torpedo-boats to come from England and third of our craft to be commissioned. I drove down to see her but could not get on board. There, before my eyes, was the Service on which I had set my heart actually in being while I was learning the best places for digging latrines near an L.O.P.. If I had waited in Dublin and kept agitating for interviews *as a civilian* I would probably have been in the Marine branch by then, and from that point of view joining the Coast Watching branch had been a mistake. I became frantic with impatience.

In the Barracks they advised me to see Chief Petty Officer Power, a meteoric ex-R.N. man, but the nearest I got to him at that time was to see a bicycle

Chief Petty Officer
(Mister) Power.

lying on the ground in Collins Barracks with the back wheel actually spinning and to be told that the Chief P.O. had just thrown it down a few seconds ago. He was living in Barracks all right, but I never contacted him.

The weeks ran quickly by Lectures, Foot drill, Field-days and 'Oliver Gore'. 'Oliver Gore' was our name for semaphore since the command in Irish which spread us out for the purpose of signalling began, 'Ollamh i gcoir –' and sounded like Oliver Gore. Everything led up to a final comprehensive examination and then suddenly it was all over and we had to depart to our L.O.P.s.

Naturally there was a 'last night', and O'Neill, Corporal Dolan and I driving back from a final evening out together ran into an interesting situation at the Barrack gate. Two officers who had been attached to the Course had – of all unlikely happenings – caught a ferret on the Quays, and had just handed it over to the quite solemn-faced Guard Commander Under Close Arrest. He refused to give it up next day since the officers could not produce a receipt for the ferret's live body.

The two officers insisted that the end of the evening had not come, made it an order in fact, and we were soon sitting in a large upstairs room in a hotel. Here the evening became slightly elaborate and at the height of the revelry the door opened and a Mr. X entered the room. This X business has nothing to do with the trawler M—— C——. I know Mr. X's real name but I fear an action for slander – even if it is fair comment, if such a thing is legally possible. Mr. X took me back a number of years to the end of an Easter Term at school and a carriageful of us returning home by the G.N.R. Somewhere – Clones probably – the door opened and Mr. X came in, accompanied by a friend. He was not long in explaining that he and friend were going off to New York to a 'card-playing championship' and would we mind if they practiced a bit? We had no objection so the two competitors spread a macintosh and went ahead with their training; the work-out was Spot The Lady. Friend very kindly showed us how maladroit his partner was by slyly indicating where the Queen was hiding. We watched friend winning with great attention. Then Mr. X generously said that it was a pity that all his young friends did not join in, so the young friends – who had seen more than one race-course – did join in. In a few minutes Mr. X's stupidity was proved for us and having been allowed to win about a pound between us we stopped playing, and when Mr. X and friend began to get difficult we told a passing ticket inspector. A very mean action, I now think.

Here was Mr. X, apparently unaltered, and full of joy at meeting the gallant boys who were serving their country – drinks all round etc. and what about a game of cards. The gallant boys agreed and I could not get a word in at all. But, as it happened, we were discussing race-courses and the art of tic-tac while waiting to start (X said he had diplomas for tic-tac) and I asked him how fast he could send a change of odds from one ring to another. He demonstrated. I said I could do it faster by semaphore and sent 'cardsharper'. The gallant boys at last understood, Mr. X was given a drink in return for his kindness and cards were forgotten. Shortly afterwards the proprietor firmly asked Mr. X to step outside and he was led away shouting an invitation to dine with him in a city hotel at his expense the following night.

When we drove home the officers insisted that the car should not only be brought into Barracks but be driven to their quarters before going on to ours, and next morning I found it impossible to drive out of the space where I had gaily parked it in the small hours without scraping the enamel off a wing,

It had been a grand Course, perfectly suited to Coast Watching needs, and the army on all those Courses showed the greatest wisdom in dealing with a Service which was more or less foreign to them.

Next morning was a day of reckoning; a day of cleaning up every single bit of the billets before the next draft arrived; a day of drawing new uniforms and a day of explaining how a car which was not officially in Barracks could receive a pass to go out again.

And then, back to the L.O.P., to one-hour-in and one-hour-out, to the sea and the sky and the rocks.

5

Suspicious Object.
Altered Course

I brought back from the Course a number of new rules and changes in routine, all those who went on Courses did so, and they were put into effect immediately. I was soon back at work again, doing chart problems or knots and splices while on my hour in. But the Post was not the same, nor were some of the crowd — in fact nothing was quite the same. I had a feeling that I was being watched and talked about, I could not believe it at first and then the corporal admitted to me that for some reason I was 'suspected'. He could not tell me anything else.

A few days afterwards a man on the Post with whom I had spent many nights, teaching him morse and semaphore dramatically accused me of being a 'spy'. Just the one word, he did not say whether he meant British or German. I complained to the District Officer at once and he told me to pay no attention to what was said. I brought the story to the Corballises and they told me that they were quite aware of the suspicion but not to worry, and what about lunch on Sunday?

I could not make it out. Now I think that perhaps someone who wanted my job started the story. Certainly it was eagerly lapped up and I had plenty of informants as to its success. Inventing and propagating rumour is a pastime of all small societies. I have known shore-rumours to be born at sea, after we had been out a couple of days on patrol. The small town of Wicklow did its job thoroughly and I often looked at its dank wharves and wished that it had a main road running through it, bringing life and movement into it and linking it along the coast with bright and charming Arklow, which has not half its advantages, scenic or otherwise.

Some people were malicious in a mean manner: a man who knew that I had been at Cambridge stopped me to tell me that the university had been bombed out of existence and watched eagerly to see how I would take his lying words.

There was nothing normal about it, nothing suggesting that people were just amusing themselves. It was furtive and spiteful.

I suppose the set-up must have been strange. What was I doing here, a foreigner (for my home is in West Wicklow) with my pay going to keep me in an hotel? That I was waiting for the Marine Service was too well known to be believed. And I was too smart at Signals, and I understood the news in French, and I used to go away on occasional week-ends. Wasn't that enough to prove a man to be a spy?

I was waiting for lunch in the hotel one day, thinking over everything, when the news of the fall of France came through. That was the worst hour of a bad nine months. So my friends in France had been right a year ago when they said that their country was doomed. To think of Normandy, and then Brittany, over-run. To think of the straight-cut military roads between the flat fields crowded with refugees – old people, and the children of the last war carrying their babies of this one. To think of those who had betrayed that splendid army, to remember those sailors I had met at Brest.

It seemed inevitable now that an invader would soon be here, and what was I doing? The nucleus of a Marine Service was already in being and I was still posted on top of a cliff, ready to report the enemy's arrival to the I.O. in the proper form, together with weather, wind and visibility – afterwards, I supposed, to throw stones at them. If I was even in an infantry battalion – and then I was called to the telephone and given orders to report to the Post and await two Intelligence Officers.

What now?

The Intelligence Officers, a commandant and a captain, sat on a wall below the Post and talked to me. I told them the whole story once again, Coast Watching as a stepping-stone to the Marine Service. They knew. They questioned me about my life before joining up, and they knew the answers too. Then they asked me to talk, and I told them just how I found myself, and the suspicion that surrounded me. That they also knew. They went away telling me to keep my mouth shut about the interview and I felt vaguely comforted.

When I went back to the hotel that evening I found them there. They had done some scouting round the town I think, and were waiting for me in a sitting room. I was asked to sit down and the captain offered me a drink. We had a heart-to-heart about Coast Watching. Then the commandant rang for a drink and we had a heart-to-heart about the Marine Service. By the end of that it was my turn to press the bell but I was full of the discipline of Collins Barracks and very much on the edge of my chair.

'Would it be all right, sir, if I ... er ...?' They nodded and I rang the bell. Shortly afterwards they rang for their car.

Two days later I was summoned to Collins Barracks for an interview, a real interview this time. A bare room with two tables, Commandant Harrington, who was O/C of the Course, is sitting at one, a Marine Service officer is at the other. I salute. Commandant Herrington passes me on to the Marine Service officer, Lieut. Thompson, and then the fun begins. Number? Name? age? I give it all gladly. What do you know? I stumble out my experience in yachts, fishing boats and trawlers prior to starting the correspondence course. What correspondence course? Give me the syllabus. I give it ... Time Azimuth, he stops me. Questions, questions. Running Fix ... he unrolls a chart and paper-clips become ships, Sextant ... its errors, please. Vertical angle, horizontal angle, Rule of the Road, Lights, Buoyage, supposing you were heading WSW ... in the event of this ... among these objects which three would you chose for a Fix? I remember that question particularly because it was the last and I did not choose the best objects.

'All right. That'll do. Wait outside.'

The door opens again and I am brought back. I am to be called up when the Service mobilises in Collins Barracks. I venture to ask when this will be and Commandant Harrington tells me, a little impatiently, that he doesn't know.

'... as to your position,' he is saying, 'the commissioned ranks are, of course, full, but ...' The *commissioned* ranks! And the most I had hoped for was A.B. I begin to mutter something and then stop myself; after all, why should I advertise my lack of ambition.

'All right, Davidson. You'll be notified shortly.'

'Thank you, sir.' I try to include both of them in my smartest and most grateful salute but they are bending over papers.

I cornered back to Wicklow on two wheels. To hell with them, and their suspicions! But there was no need of that. Small-town gossip had done it again and it was well known that I had sat for an hour in the hotel with two Intelligence Officers. 'Spy indeed ... sure that fellow's a ... didn't I always say ...' I was given all details of the *volte face* by my friend the corporal. Sergeant Turner had left us for Sligo long previously.

Impatience possessed me now. Rush to examine the mails every morning ... call up friendly N.C.O.s at Collins Barracks ... pester the District Officer ...

And then suddenly O'Neill was told to pack up and report to Collins Barracks for clerical work. Dolan and I had pursuaded [sic] him to apply for a transfer. Something must be going to happen now, and soon, it *must* be soon.

The weather was glorious, a reward for all our hardships of the winter. We shed our great-coats and spent all the time out of doors watching the convoys. Equally perfect were the calm nights when the land gave off the heat it had soaked up during the day. A new diversion was the Code of Rings which simultaneously connected every Post in the Command with Dublin. It began with a mysterious, sealed and secret box being installed in the telephone exchange and nightly rehearsals started. One number of rings indicated that all Posts were on to Dublin, another number was for our Post alone and when the switch was in we were only to use the phone on receiving our Code of Rings, except in a case of emergency. The system worked very well in the end.

One morning we were waiting to be relieved after an interesting night-watch, loud with aircraft and gun-fire at sea. The ground was now so dry that I could drive the car to the very top of the cliff and I climbed down the ladder and switched on the car-radio to wait for the news. What a lovely morning, I thought, stretching myself sleepily. Then something happened which seemed so cinematic and appropriate that one almost laughed. As the radio warmed up the reiterated four notes of Grieg's so-well-known *Morning* came from it, growing in volume and breadth of chording as the sun rose from the morning clouds in the east and struck full on me through the windshield. Inexpressible moment with the sun leaving the sea and rising to the glowing and guile-less *Morning*. Suddenly everything seemed to come right. The morning, the music and the sun were right – everything was indescribably right and something good must surely happen!

We signed over to the next Watch and drove off. I dropped Patchell off near his own house, bought a paper, and sat down to breakfast. Letters on my table – an official letter!

'You have been appointed to the rating of Chief Petty Officer (Torpedo Coxswain) in the Marine Service ...'

It was beyond belief! Chief Petty Officer!

'If you intend to take up this appointment you should report before 11.00 hrs tomorrow ...'

If I *intend*! When do I report, and where? Collins Barracks, to-morrow. Then I'll leave at once.

My bill! I called for my bill. What did it matter if I had been up all night. I packed.

'All that lot down in the hall at once, please. I'll be back in half an hour.'

I drove out to Corporal O'Sullivan and pushed the summons into his hand and we said our good-byes while I watched the promise of the morning grow to certainty from the heights of Ballyguile.

I decided to say nothing to the Coast Watching Service. I would assume that they knew about my appointment. If I phoned them I might be told to wait on the Post until they had been officially notified. No, better make a mistake than lose an opportunity through being too *wording* scrupulous.

A good-bye here, a good-bye there. Now my suitcase, typewriter, kit-bag, clothing-bag, rubber boots and greatcoat are in the car. I switch on and ease the gear-lever into bottom. The gravel crunches as I roll from the hotel.

Baaarp! go the twin horns as I reach the road. I accelerate and change up, accelerate again and change into top. The warm wind is singing past my ears in the open car and I settle my cap more firmly on my head. Wicklow Town falls behind me; Coast Watching falls behind me; the cold, the fog, mist, falling snow and heavy rain-storms are forgotten.

One stop. I turn in to Rosanna. The Corballises are all away. No, Captain Corballis is at home and he sets a whiskey and soda before me with his congratulations. But, he says — looking me straight in the eye, the British are going to invade here next Monday. What an awkward time they have chosen, I think. Still, it's three days off. I won't bite for information. Then the smiling villain leads me away to see his air-raid shelter.

Don't forget Monday! he shouts as I drive off.

Much about Monday! I rushed on to Dublin, on to George in the Buttery before lunch, what a place to change feet at!

One little thing worried me. My summons was for to-morrow. What was I doing, enjoying myself round town in this manner. Of course! I'd been on watch all night, I had forgotten that. It was my free time and normally I should have been resting. So I went home for the night.

Another little thing worried me, this appointment as Torpedo Coxswain. As far as Navigation and Seamanship went I could make a sort of a stab at the Chief P.O. side of the job, but what was a Torpedo Coxswain? What was a torpedo, if it came to that, outside of being a cigar-shaped object liable to go off with a bang? Next morning, therefore, I breakfasted with volume SWA-ZYR of the encyclopedia open before me at Torpedo. Though a very recent encyclopedia it was much out of date on this subject and I finished breakfast with a confused impression of Defended Harbours, gun-cotton, compressed air and rams.

Collins Barracks again. 'Marine Service,' I muttered to the P.A. admitting me. In the Orderly Room I was told to see Commandant Harrington. Commandant Harrington told me in, I felt, a slightly surprised way, that I had been selected as a Chief Petty Officer, that he hoped I would make a success of it and that I must be prepared '… to undergo a course or courses of instruction in Torpedoes, about which — of course — you know nothing.'

Nothing! Come now, Commandant, that's going a bit far; there are degrees of ignorance and after all I had interrupted my breakfast to read up Torpedoes. Nothing, indeed!

'Yes, sir,' I saluted and went away.

The next face before me was O'Neill's and he gravely led me through a questionnaire about my past life and details of bankruptcies or family lunacy that I might like to offer. Then I signed the answers.

'Well, Davidson,' another face, Company-Sergeant Maher, he who had offered us *word-all* for tea, was shaking hands with me.

'Good-morning, sir.'

'Don't say "sir",' muttered O'Neill, 'you're equal ranks now.' A moment later Sergeant Harpur – one of my late instructors – sirred me and everything became a bit vertiginous.

The C.S. said it was time for lunch and my mind jumped to a parade. I murmured something about my plate, mug, knife, fork and spoon and was told that I belonged to the Sergeant's Mess now, where all these things were provided. I then decided that I really must be a C.P.O.

My greatest shock came when my kit was brought into the billets which I had occupied a few months previously. I say *brought* in because my first act of authority was to find out which men were seamen (we all in civvies) and detail two of them to carry it there. To my relief, they obeyed.

The floor, in whose washing and sweeping I had so often assisted, was covered with dry mud. In place of the perfectly aligned bed-boards and rolled bedding the beds were made down and pulled about anyway. Suitcases were thrown here and there or heaped on the shelves where our orderly kits had shone, and the tremendous noise was momentarily hushed as I was sourly inspected. It did not take me long to find out that the Adjutant-General's writ did not run, as far as the Marine Service in formation was concerned, and that night I saw the Barrack Orderly, who had come to complain about lights burning after Lights Out, being rushed out of the room with many suggestions as to what he could do with himself.

So there we were, the yachtsmen, the fishing men, the couple-of-voyages deep sea men, the chancers, the genuine deep sea men who made oases of order around them, and the starkly and blindly inexperienced. I sat down and began to take stock of those around me while they looked at this addition to the Petty Officers. There was Kinsella of Arklow, a real deep-sea man – one of the crew of a dry-docked Patrol-vessel – silent and none too pleased with his surroundings. There was Con McCarthy, a giant of an engineer C.P.O. who delighted in hurling a 56lb cannon-ball from one end of the room to the other. Dick Cotter, whom I grew to know best of them, another C.P.O. – a yachtsman and our resident comedian. Jack Bellamy, an engineer petty Officer. C.P.O. Tom Alsop, a yachtsmen already worried about our lack of organisation. And Nick.

If I devoted the rest of this book to C.P.O. Nick Kennedy I could not create him for you because he is too elusive and his sayings come too rapidly and are of too 'Service' an interest to be written down. He was a tall, youngish Co. Wexford man who seemed to have served in a great many ships and to have unedifying stories about most of them. Later I found that he is capable of doing anything up to the point of actual crime, and he can get away with it too. Nick's idea it was to exhume a dead dog, white-wash it and leave it on the deck of a torpedo-boat in the moonlight to greet its owner.

'I never laughed as much in my life,' Nick once said to me, describing how a Chinese work-man had fallen off a staging to the bottom of a dry-dock in Shanghai. I reproved him and he said, 'Ah, it wasn't the fellow's fall that made me laugh, it was when his mates put red-lead on him for an antiseptic.'

From the very start of the Service Nick came right out as a really reliable leader in whatever he undertook. Later on we found the sheets showing what impressions we had created at the interview

Nick Kennedy.

I have described as occurring some months ago. 'An excellent type' it said of Nick, and his character could not have been more precisely put.

His present amusement, however, was upsetting the deep sea stories of the 'chancers' and picking out of the crowd those whom he described as 'broken-down aristocrats'.

When I arrived the Service had already been formed for a few weeks, and after the last of the stream of recruits had been attested all were waiting for the move to the Base; some said it would be Haulbowline, others knew it would be Dunlaoghaire. The routine among the Chief P.O.s and P.O.s was to rise for a late breakfast, go to bed again; rise for lunch, sleep again or play cards; rise for tea and then spend the evening in the city. Strange were the doings at night, strange the behaviour of Jack Bellamy when he asked us to help him to turn his father's car upside down outside the billets, strange and sudden the rumble of Con's cannon-ball in the night.

In the end it was outraged army officers who put an end to the maddest of those early days when they entered the billets at ten o'clock and found the C.P.O.s sleeping off the fatigues of breakfast. This was too much. An immediate issue of army boots and blue dungarees was made and the C.P.O.s had to join the men on the square at nine every morning after that, learning how to form double and single file and later how to slope their arms by numbers. In all moments of crisis or when men look unemployed, the army either declares a Test of Elementary Training or puts them on the Square and this was the army's first effort towards the creation of good order and military discipline amongst us.

But why the Barrack square for sailors? That bothered us more than a little. I think the answer is that a spell on the Barrack square assists in welding any body of men together and most men who are going to be of any use at all will emerge as competent on the square, though I have seen exceptions to this. That it teaches quickness of thinking I doubt: quick reaction to certain commands, probably, but the possible evolutions in Foot Drill and Arms Drill are limited and the emergencies of the sea are infinite. Its main usefulness was in imparting a sorely needed smart bearing to the recruits and making it clear that an order was meant to be obeyed.

During this time many of the Dublin men had sleeping-out passes and used to come in every morning. Among them was a little fair-haired fellow who seemed exceptionally young and exceptionally light-weight. If there is ever any rowing at our Depot, I remember deciding, that man will make a first-rate coxswain. He had savage blue eyes and his name was John Cashin. He was my first coxswain and I have never met better.

Because of my previous Course I was not required to go on the Square, though sometimes I assisted by walking through the ranks importantly, pushing stomachs in and correcting Slopes. I spent most of my time at work again, plodding on through the navigation course, and things settled down to a fairly regular routine, though the disorder in the billets was unchecked. I have always noticed that when one does settle down to accepting a routine existence so as to be almost unaware of its regular rhythm then something crops up to awaken one. What woke us was the Port Control.

This was a Service operating in Dublin Bay for the examination of incoming ships. It was run by soldiers, but as soon as marine matters began to become a little coherent in Collins Barracks five or six C.P.O.s and P.O.s were told off to act as coxswains in the examination launches, and each C.P.O. on duty was assisted by a man from the Army Air Corps. These were Privates Lynch, Doyle, MacLarnon, and Sergeant Gilligan. They had all done courses in elementary navigation and seamanship at Gosport as well as getting instruction in the engines of their craft. Doyle and MacLarnon and Gilligan were transferred to

Port control inspection party.

the Marine Service and at the time of writing are respectively Petty Officer
(E.R.A.) and Chief Petty Officers (Torpedo Coxswains).

The launches were Power Boats. One was a sea-plane tender and the other
– and I had heaps of experience of her – was a target-boat for aircraft. Most of
her was covered by a heavy bullet-proof canopy and her driving and steering
cockpit was entered through a watertight door. Once inside it was a matter
of wriggling to the coxswain's seat, which was rather like the cockpit of an
aircraft, with just as complicated an array of levers and dials. A small aperture
gave visibility of about one point on either bow and behind was another small
aperture looking astern. Communication with the deck or conversation inside
was quite impossible when sitting on top of the roaring engines, and the atmosphere was thick. She was quite unsuited to the task we gave her.

Each coxswain used to take over one or other craft at 8 a.m. or p.m. at the
North Wall, with the Boarding Officer and an examination party of armed and
most apprehensive soldiers detailed for the job. Then followed the ritual of The
Cap. I think it was Con McCarthy, the engineer, who originally provided The
Cap, a peaked merchant-service one. Wearing The Cap, one felt a little less of a
civilian. Wearing The Cap, dungarees and sea-boots one felt almost naval. Even
so, as we drove down the Quays on our lorry to take up duty, we always looked
like political prisoners with an escort of soldiers, and that is what the crowds at
O'Connell Bridge used to take us for. The examination party and officer were
based on the Dublin Bay Pilot Vessel at that time and in fair weather the launch

stayed out with them. On the return to the North Wall the coxswain used to hand on The Cap to his relief.

One morning when I had just turned in after being on the night examination party I heard loud discussion in the billets (there was no respect for the 'watch below') about a man who was to join the Port Control that day. He was, it appeared, at least a duke, had about six Christian names and was a golf champion. Putting two and two together I asked Paddy O'Neill to bring His Grace to see me when he reported. I was right. At eleven o'clock I was roused by the six feet and eight inches of Petty-Officer The Hon: Patrick Campbell. He had heard that I was likely to be found somewhere in the Barracks and I gave him a lot of information until it was time for him to go to the Square. When the *Maritime Magazine* began publication it was those early days that Campbell seized on and got the most amusing aspects of it. My small amount of previous service had made me sometimes a little priggish and pained about the general craziness of things but he was able to be entirely objective.

Our best and most enduring diversion at that time, and at all times, was, and is, the 'buzz', the 'Galley-buzz', the 'ball-hop', 'the Switch rumour', the 'After-peak radio', the 'Clerk in Division's yarn' and 'what a fellow out of the Orderly Room heard the Commandant say'. One popular story was that we were buying armed trawlers in Lisbon. This was killed by a second story which gave out that they had been turned down owing to being infested with bugs. These news items gave our base as Dun Laoghaire, Haulbowline or nowhere-at-all because there wasn't going to be any Marine Service, it was all knocked on the head. And then, quite suddenly, a detachment was formed, dressed in Marine Service uniform, issued with their kits, armed, and sent to England for M.T.B. *M2*. The balls hopped again, higher and higher, posting us to various M.T.B.s yet to come. We were measured for our uniforms and then things quieted down again to work on our first mines (made in a Dublin dockyard), to Port Control and to the Square.

'I don't know if you're interested,' said Chief P.O. Tom Alsop to me one day, 'but we're stripping a depth-charge pistol in the billets.' It was the first time I had spoken to him and I *was* interested, both because of the D-C pistol and because Alsop was in the habit of spending hours with Chief P.O. Power, whom I had failed to meet five months ago – in fact he was Mr. Power's Head Boy. Stripping this pistol, which sets off the ignitor in a depth-charge, was fairly easy to do with a diagram, but the correct re-assembly was another matter, and the final adjustment was another matter still. Tom could not do it and I could not even begin to attempt it. I sat on my bed and worked at the wretched thing.

'Jesus Christ and General Jackson!' shouted someone, and the D-C pistol was jerked out of my hand. 'Who told you to fiddle with that, who gave it to you?

That thing's valuable – you've no right to go messing around with what you don't understand!'

Standing over me was a burly middle-aged man with a ruddy face and blazing eyes. This must be Mr. Power.

'God almighty – the minute my back's turned – who are you, anyway?'

'C.P.O. Davidson.'

'Chief P.O! Oh, that's different, why didn't you tell me? That's a very complicated piece of mechanism you have there, I'll be starting classes on that lot quite soon. Keep on trying, we'll keep that pistol for demonstration purposes. Tom, type seven copies of this for me, I have to go up to G.H.Q. and I'll be back in an hour.'

With a whirl of words he was gone, and that was Mr. Power.

That evening Nick Kennedy came over and sat down on my bed.

'I'll be goddamed [sic] if I can make head or tail of this stuff,' he said, throwing down the type-written copies of elementary torpedo-instruction with which we had been issued.

'It's tough to get hold of.' I was brooding over mine too.

'It bloody is. Hydro-what-do-you-call-them valves and *wording* gyroscopes. I've been too long at sea to swallow that tack.'

But with a few weeks of our arrival in the Depot Nick had his hands on a torpedo and in a couple of years Mr. Power admitted that Nick knew as much about torpedoes as he did.

Suddenly we were told that our Depot at Haulbowline was ready to be taken over. The launches were to leave for the South with a small crew in each, most of the crowd would travel down by lorry, and I was told to wait on as Marine Service N.C.O. in charge of the last party to leave Collins Barracks (we called it the Demolition Squad) and, unofficially, to remove the hundred last things in my car.

I asked about petrol. It was an un-official job and a private car but I had done plenty of semi-duty running about in it both here and in the Coast Watching time. As it happened, we were refuelling the launches that afternoon.

'I suppose you could have some,' was the reply, after immense thought and chin-rasping.

'How much, sir?

'As much as your conscience allows you in the circumstances.'

When we had completed refuelling the launches a ten-gallon drum remained in the lorry.

'How much petrol would your conscience allow you, in the circumstances?' I asked Pte. MacLarnon.

'Ten gallons,' said MacLarnon and Doyle without hesitation. The night before the main body of the Service was due to leave Paddy Campbell came in to see me from the Port Control's new permanent quarters at Alexandre Basin. He had red-hot news. Anthony Eden had flown over to see An Taoiseach and demand the return of the Ports. If he was refused he would fly back and Britain would invade. Proving everything of course, an aircraft passed over the Barracks. Really it was a bit hard, we said, that an invasion should begin before we had reached our Depot, let alone got afloat.

Next morning the whole Marine Service detachment loaded live ammunition for the first time. The lorries were drawn up and ready for the long run down to Cobh, the cooks had gone ahead to make a roadside meal near Cahir. The hours on the square were showing results and the Service, though still in civilian attire, was drawn up with some regard for bearing, covering and dressing. C/S Maher brought them to attention, sloped their arms, hoped it would be all right, and handed them over to the Commanding Officer. He inspected them, inspected their rifles and then it came.

'Ten rounds ... standing ... charge magazines!'

Those of us who were not in the detachment moved to the shelter of the waiting lorries. Officers and army N.C.O.s walked anxiously through the ranks to ensure that as the bolts went home they were not pushing rounds up the breech. But everything went perfectly.

And then they were in the lorries, cheering the party left behind, cheering the P.A.s at the gate, cheering the road ahead.

Something had started.

The last days we spent in Dublin were amusing. My demolition squad was loading stores and I enjoyed this because, subject to the approval of an officer who rarely troubled me, I had control over a goods-train in a siding.

The question of a bronze propellor-shaft came up. It was lying beside a huge lorry fitted with a crane in Collins Barracks. Would I have one or two flat bogeys for it? The foreman explained matters and talked about 'the road'. From him I learned that to do the job really properly two bogeys would be needed but that it might be done with one. Hesitating about spending an extra flat-bogey's worth of the Poor Farmer's money (we always called it that) I phoned my officer and found that the lorry and crane had gone away and the propellor-shaft did not interest us any more since it was immovable.

This was an early lesson to me in the folly of assuming anything in the Service without a statement in writing. And later on I would have known that even had the lorry been there it might have required an Act in the Dail to permit Transport, or whoever owned the lorry, to facilitate us.

Paddy Campbell came down to Donard with me to complete the job of closing it and handing it over to a caretaker and he let his imagination go in the matter of extra gear I thought of bringing. This and this and most certainly *this* would be invaluable to me in the Marine Service and at the moment of writing there are still some of Campbell's essentials in my laid-up car; a leather bag something like a shopping bag with a zip-fastener, a skiing helmet and a copy of a Breton autonomist paper, a souvenir which he discovered.

Then one morning I started for Cobh accompanied by one of the army sergeants attached to the Service, and with the back of the car and the luggage boot full of our kit and all the forgotten things out of the Orderly Room. I did not know that I should have had a pass to take all this gear out of Barracks. The P.A. at the gate peered suspiciously at the typewriters and bulging cases of files.

'Marine Service,' said Sergt Cooney. The P.A. sighed resignedly, they were very glad to see us go. Then he recognised me from the Coast Watcher's Course.

'Would you mind telling me what in the name of God you are now?' he said.

6

Altered Course South

After a hundred and sixty miles driving we swept down the hill and drew up in Cobh.

The town of Cobh looks best from the harbour because it rises too sharply from the sea to be seen comprehensively ashore. This view from the harbour was one which I was to know very well in the ensuing years. In steep streets and terraces, with many-coloured houses fighting to hold on to the precipitous slope, it climbs from the waterfront up to the great Cathedral, and beyond it. I am often tantalised by not knowing whether I like the Cathedral or not. Gleaming wet after a shower it is lovely: silhouetted in fog it broods over the town, as massive as it was light and airy before; but in the full glare of a cloudless sky it seems hard and precise and spiky yet it has an authority which draws and holds the eye.

Cobh as seen from Haulbowline.

Cobh is on one of the islands which are in Cork Harbour, it is connected with the mainland by a short bridge and its insularity is not apparent, except on the remarkably lovely train-run up to Cork, but the gibe at settlers in Cobh is, 'You only came in over Belvelly Bridge.' Other islands are Little Island, Fota Island, Haulbowline, Rocky Island and the celebrated Spike Island. It was in Spike that we were quartered at present. The last detachment had arrived by train and those who had gone ahead were ashore too. I sat down with the crowd in the Westbourne and the place was in an uproar, everyone trying to tell the absurd things that had happened – and all at the same time too. For instance, the two launches had entered the harbour at low water. Coming round the Spit light-house they decided to make a spectacular dash together towards the pier at Spike Island, and so they did, but it was only 'towards' Spike Island because they had not reckoned on an intervening bank upon which they ran up together with military precision. I could continue almost indefinitely with stories of the amusing side of our life; gather any body of strangers together and sooner or later they will be talking about the amusing things that their being together has caused, but this would not give a true picture of the Service, nor would the tale of, say, Batt and the second depth-charge have any interest outside the Service.

Looking back on those wild days I think we behaved extremely badly ashore. There were no uniforms, all ranks mixed together, we were noisy and we were quite without discipline. The people of Cobh did not like us a bit though they did admit that we were a little better behaved than the American sailors in the last war. But in the ensuing years we redeemed ourselves in their eyes and became, in a sense, their own. One cause for this was that the Service married happily and in large numbers into the town, Dublin men, Kerry men, Donegal

Department of Defence vessel *John Adams* service to Haulbowline and Spike.

men and Arklow men. Cobh has never wanted for new blood and we brought our tributaries to the stream. It says a great deal for the charm of the girls of Co. Cork that once a man became at all tangled up he very seldom escaped. Now, when I see a man getting a wandering look in his eyes and seeking lots of shore-leave I automatically begin to think of the inevitable sequence of events that lies ahead; the Permission to get Married, the Leave, the Wedding Present, then the Solemnisation of Matrimony (verified), the Admission to the Married Establishment, the Entitlement to Continuous Ration Allowance when at anchor, the Change of Home Address, the change of next of kin from Father to Wife, then a period of calm until the Granting of Special Leave (Serious illness of Immediate Relative. Wife) and the announcement of the birth of a Son. Patrick. Joseph. (verified). And still, regardless of the trouble they give, they keep on marrying.

Late that night one of the Department of Defence vessels, used for carrying troops, stores, and for towing targets for the Artillery, took us to Spike, circling round grim, lightless, derelict, menacing Haulbowline.

The entrance to Spike Island fort.

One might say, rather extravagantly, that from the heights of Cobh the island of Spike looks like a cut emerald set in the blue enamel of the harbour. But from the decks of a D.O.D. boat at night the lovely harbour just looks like water and Spike looks like a lump of island, and an uninviting one at that.

We carried our kits up a winding road cut into the hillside. We crossed a drawbridge over a dry moat and passed under a frowning archway inscribed 'Fort Westmorland 1838' and entered the Fort through a tunnel and a barred gate. Inside my impression

An indication of the condition of the accommodation for the Marine Service with which Norris and company were presented on moving to Haulbowline in 1940. This building became the Non Commissioned Officers' mess, 'Our Mess' in Norris's account.

was of immensity and gloom. There were very few lights and it was impossible for me to imagine my surroundings in the darkness. The top of Spike Island was flattened off and dug down so that a Barracks might be built below the level of the lip, on which the guns were, of the resulting crater. Around this lip, the immensely thick walls, ran the dry moat, and from the other side of that the island sloped down to the sea. The only view one sees in Fort Westmoreland is the sky, unless one climbs up out of the crater to the guns.

Dick Cotter led me away to a sort of room, or large cell, which I was to share with him. It was in a dank block and was said to have been John Mitchel's room, but so was every other rabbit-burrow under the walls of the fort. A little water dribbled down the plaster facing of the stone-walled room. Many an irreverent conversation Dick and I had with the shade of the great Mitchel, Dick doing the part of Mitchel as well as his own and answering all our complaints with, 'Ah, but you should have been here in the time of the British.' Our cell was only temporary and were soon moved into really good quarters. Immediately after breakfast we were called out on the square and our C.S. approached us in a way that showed that he was little pleased with the goings-on of the night before. Naturally he set us to forming Single and Double File when Advancing, not to mention when Retiring. We carried this out with more than our usual clumsiness because we were wearing rubber boots. Then we were taken off to the boat again and landed in the Basin at Haulbowline. Convict labour had built that Basin and we often felt that we were re-living the past.

This very early period of ours in Haulbowline was full of interest. First, the island itself, and its name. There is a very doubtful story that it got its name from hauling on bowlines in order to warp a vessel to a dockside, or something like that. I don't believe a word of it. How would that explain Haulbowline in Carlingford Lough? Personally I believe it comes from *arod bullaun*; a *bullaun* being, I am told, a rock which usually has a hollow at the top which might

Haulbowline, as seen from Cobh, early twentieth century. In the late 1930s Irish Steel occupied the main dockyard workshop area, around the high sheerleg crane.

hold water. Well, the top of Haulbowline is rock and there are, at least, puddles there. Furthermore, the two Haulbowlines and Ardboline off Sligo, are of similar shape, and so it all seems to fit nicely except that the local Irish name for Haul bowline is not *Ard Bullaun*, it is *Inis Sionnac*, the island of the foxes. I have consulted Joyce and others and I cannot get beyond this, but I do not believe in the hauling of bowlines derivation, it seems strained – like the inn-sign of The Goat And Compasses which is explained as God Encompass Us (who would call a pub that, anyhow?) and the Fantastic derivation of Kinsale as meaning 'King sail' because James the second sailed from there.

Haulbowline is a high cliff to the west and north and drops down to the flat reclamations of the south and east. When we came there was, at the west end, a pier, some derelict civilian houses and a few immense warehouses. At the top of the cliff were rows of abandoned married quarters, a ball-alley and a Martello tower. There was also a school-house which we converted into a laundry. Indeed, conversion is a feature of the Service. Apart from the conversion of civilians into sailors with an unwillingly absorbed military flavour, we also converted soldiers into sailors – some of them in name only – and any small-craft we laid hands on were turned into something different. Just after the signing of the Treaty an Irish naval service had existed here for some time but the fleet of armed trawlers was eventually sold and converted back into fishing trawlers. There were many stories about this service and some of the buildings were still faintly stamped with the names of the offices into which they had been temporarily converted. Roads and a railway led across the island to where the great naval dockyard had been, but now the only ship-repairing was done by a yacht-builder who had converted part of the original Mast House. Near here was one of the many fine buildings in the island (we converted it into a very good canteen) and right in the centre were what might have been two sides of a demure city square built about a tangled tennis court. Everywhere there were evidences of other days, in the tales of those who lived in the island and in the quarters named after ships; Hero Row and Leander Row. At the top of everything was a derelict Signal Station; below it, an Oil Refinery. Intervening between this and the Steel Works were more warehouses, very handsome limestone buildings. Beyond all that was the Basin and the Graving Dock.

Rusty machinery, rotting caissons, scrap from the wreck of the *Celtic*; long-necked, despondent-looking cranes, weeds growing thickly, except where the civilian families lived, carpets of dust in every building. This is what we had to get down to. This is what we had to clean up so that the infant Service might breathe, had to bring life into all this.

I often wondered whether we could do it when I saw the faint traces of the service that had been there before us and when I looked at the ruins of the Dockyard and Engineering Shops, whose contents had been sold for scrap. There is a saying that nothing can ever succeed in Haulbowline because of the convicts' forced labour which went to its building. What chance had we of breathing life into these massive and decaying bones?

Well, my first effort at inducing life was to take charge of a white-washing party – with a brush in my own hand too.

★ ★ ★

As I write my ship is lying in the Basin and I have just come back from our Mess, the Orderly Room and offices of the 1922 service. There was a bright fire of wood and turf in a huge brick grate with a few chairs beside it. Earlier in the evening a table was taken up by card players and another group was listening to the *Itma* programme. At the same time drinks were coming across the bar and here and there were some staid and respected civilians, honorary members of the Mess in whose eyes we each had our degree of standing – the very 'time of the British' fathers who had looked with little approval on the wild hordes of five years ago. Now only a few of us remained and we were breaking up. Outside, lights shone in the re-built warehouses which were now billets. There were lights in the School of Navigation, too, and in the re-conditioned houses which looked down across a terrace of grass and flowers to the Parade Ground and the Gymnasium, the Rifle Range and the School of Gunnery. Lights in the huge block of the Supplies Stores showed that they must be working on a check.

I walked away along the tarmac which now covered the rutted track and railway lines of other days. I walked below the artificial slope covered with green sods brought from Spike, under the arch and past the massive colonnade of the Men's Canteen.

'Halt!' A sentry; steel helmet, heavy blue greatcoat, black bandolier and gleaming white-web leggings. I say good-night as I pass him.

'Good-night, sir.' A good lad: one of the Rowing Club.

More lights outside the East Gate. Lights in the Officers' Mess and in the warehouses (now billets) where the M.T.B. crews off duty, and the Construction Corps, sleep. Lights and life in the island.

I go on round the Basin and past the dark silhouette of the new Mast House. As I walk down the East Wall I am halted again by a sentry on his beat above the pontoons to which the motor torpedo-boats are made fast. My ship lies along-side the Fitting Shop. I go aboard, drink a cup of cocoa and turn in. Everything is normal. Everything is smoothly running. Here and there in parts of the island which we do not control there is still a heap of rusting machinery or a patch of weeds. But, as for ourselves, we are *au point*, we have come a long way.

Complacency? Far from it. I made this walk to-night with feelings of the greatest uneasiness and dissatisfaction, but what could still please me was that the order of things had not been outwardly disturbed by what was happening, that we were maintaining the standard to which we had progressed. I will return to this evening at the end of the book.

★ ★ ★

Whitewashing was not my only job. Regardless of qualifications, everyone had to do everything, and men were emerging; he's good, he's good if you keep after him, he's useless, he's a chancer – I think the chancers were the most unpopular. We were not at sea yet and some of us never got to sea, but even the proximity of the sea seemed to have its effect. It is an acid which etches out the whole man before the eyes of his shipmates, the sea will eventually show whether he can or cannot perform the task it sets him.

But at that time no one expected very much of anyone because, though we were beginning to get ourselves sorted out and identified, no one knew by virtue of what qualifications a man held his rating. For some time Tom Alsop and I worked on large sheets which listed the personnel of each of our few craft, and those to come. But I gladly gave way to Tom's exquisite lettering one day when I got a sudden call to the Basin. It had been remembered that I was one of the coxswains of the launches and the Target Boat's mid-engine was cutting out. Dick Cotter was put on the job with me, and what did either of us know about it? We decided to take out the erring engine and replace it with an identical one from the sea-plane tender which was up for repairs. We unscrewed everything in sight, parted all the fuel lines and then – four hands to the crane – heave away! An engine swings up in the air and is landed on the quayside. Lower away! Another engine swings down and settled on its bearers. Now, this should screw on here, and this must screw on there, and this ought to go here – doesn't look quite right somehow but it fits – let's try it anyway. No bother!

Fortunately we found a Petty Officer called Tim Gillan who turned out to be an E.R.A. and he probably prevented us from doing a lot of damage.

Now-a-days Marine Transport would probably have to notify the Depot that the Target Boat was out of service. Next, there would be a Requisition to the Fitting Shop for the removal and repair of the engine. Then, after deliberation, a careful removal, probably assisted by civilian employees.

Perhaps that's the safer and better way, but the way Dick and I did it was the only possible way and we frequently invoked the shade of Mitchel for advice. As regards engines, we were out-and-out chancers, but chancers *malgre nous* –

Transport had to be kept running for we were an island, and how would the officers manage to get their lunch in Spike if the Target Boat did not run?

We used to eat sausage sandwiches and drink mugs of tea round a Corporal cooker at mid-day and we had our big meal when returned to Spike.

Another little interlude was the Wire Splice. Major (now Colonel) Anthony Lawlor, our then Director, was leaving the sea-plane tender one day and pointed out that one of the stays was very slack. C.P.O. Good and I found that we could not set up the bottle-screws any harder, and that the wire had rusted round the thimbles, so we decided to fit a new stay, and we made that simple job last for three days as the weather was bad. It became known to the C.S. that we were working on some very esoteric branch of seamanship.

'Fall out the C.P.O.s doing that wire-splice!' he would say each morning when we fell in after landing in the island from Spike.

We used to shut ourselves up in the Blacksmith's Shop and talk about M.T.B.s to come, if and when. Our enormous task was to splice two thimbles into inch and a quarter wire rope. As I say, we made the job last for three days and at the end of that time we produced two revolting splices which had to be hastily hammered into shape and served. Our retreat was soon discovered and became popular with those wanting a quiet smoke. One morning the Blacksmith's Shop suddenly rang with activity. One man blew the forge furiously, another hammered idiotically on the anvil and others grabbed the wire and fiddled while Bob Good and I worked. Commandant Harrington and some officers had entered the Shop to see what was going on. Someone had spotted them and all backs were industriously bent over imaginary tasks when they came in. It was the usual set-up, men so hard at work that they were simply unconscious of an officer's approach until he speaks.

'You all seem to be very busy,' said the Commandant, but he italicised the *seem* and that was the last day of the wire-splice racket. As it happened, the Blacksmith's Shop did not belong to us at all, it was Board of Works property – as was much of the island – we had no right to be there. But that was the way of things in those days. We were like very young children who have yet to learn that their parents do not own everything in sight.

Sergeant Harpur once opened a store and showed me a staggering collection of blocks, tackles and purchases but I soon found out that the Marine Service didn't own them, in fact we owned almost nothing. So, arising from our wants, came the Requisitions, and aiming at their fulfillment came the Technical and other Stores, building up stocks according to the various demands. But, though we owned little, there was still so much gear lying round the island, even after the sale of the Naval Dockyard, that we had a saying that anything could be found provided one searched long enough. A little speed-dinghy had a habit of throwing its starting handle over the side. Someone found a starting handle rusting in the grass and 'dogs' were fitted to it – Blacksmith's Shop job, that. A few days later she threw that handle away with a backfire; I found a derelict lorry and soon she had a handle again.

After a bit we had a sort of Ration Stores, a kind of Office, what passed for a Medical Hut, and a room for the Commanding Officer. There was no telephone. M.T.B. *M.1*, which lay in the Basin, had a telephone to the shore and messages between the Office and the telephone were usually conveyed by means of the invaluable Oliver Gore.

Something else was also being supplied according to the demand – Law. To begin with we had no rules at all. When we arrived in Spike we had to conform to the Barracks routine. Now, every offence caused its appropriate countermeasure to be taken, earths were being stopped and we began to hear about the Defence Force Temporary Provisions Act 1923/40. Night about we had to take turns at being Marine Service Duty Petty Officer (we refused the army term 'Orderly Sergeant'), meeting each crowd coming back from Cobh at night.

So the preliminaries continued; whitewashing, scrubbing, running the launches, and our nights ashore playing the piano in the Imperial Hotel and talking endlessly about the M.T.B.s to come and listening to red-hot information, and believing it too.

Muirchu anchored off Cobh.

Then one day two officers left us, with C.P.O. Good and a crew, to bring back *M.3* and a few days afterwards the *Muirchu*, No. 1 Patrol-Vessel came in. I was on duty in Spike the night she came in and her Chief P.O., C.P.O. Flannery, landed in Spike before going on leave next day. Flannery held a Foreign Mates's [sic] ticket and had accepted C.P.O. rating pending a commission. When I was showing him where he would sleep he mentioned that he thought I was going to join the ship next day. Nick Kennedy was already serving on her but the possible move annoyed me a little because I felt that it might prevent me from joining *M.5*, for which M.T.B. I was intended. But meanwhile, if I was going to her, there was an awful lot for me to find out, so I asked him for a rough idea of what one's duties were, and what the routine was. Our beds were adjoining. 'Oh ... just the usual, you know,' said Flann, easily, 'Third Mate's Job.' But I didn't know. I didn't know anything.

'I mean,' I said, 'what do I do, say, when we're going out?'

'Same as any other ship.' He wasn't being helpful at all, he was accepting me as a seaman familiar with his duties instead of as a sort of converted yachtsmen. So I explained.

'Ah,' he said; lighting a cigarette and considering, 'I see. Got a bit of paper?' And then he gave me the facts of life as lived in a patrol-vessel, quarters, mess, duties, and the answer to anything I could think of asking him.

I'm afraid my ideas of the *Muirchu* in those days were based on comic papers and pantomime jokes. It was this, and the possibility of being put out of line for an M.T.B., and the separation from the crowd in which I was settling down, that displeased me but I noted down everything I did not understand – that's to say I noted down everything. It would be a change from our daily trips to work on building up our Depot, and from running the launches. Anyhow it was only a buzz.

But next day Captain O'Connor sent for me and told me to report on board the *Muirchu*.

'Razor ...' I ventured.

'No time. The crew's here now drawing kit. You're sailing immediately.'

The crew were sitting in the ship's dinghy, more of them were in the sea-plane tender which was towing her and all were hugging bundles of their new kit which would replace their Department of Fisheries uniforms. When we reached the hulk to which the *Muirchu* was made fast the coalies were being knocked off work. We were being rushed out. There was a scare on, the first of many. Something resembling a troop-ship, nationality unknown and apparently black with soldiers, was reported as proceeding along the coast. *M.1* went roaring out as we cast off, leaving a broad and foaming trail behind her down the channel. The ship was due for rations that day, nearly everything was out, and there were no rations at all for me. All I had was what I wore, rubber boots and dungarees, not even The Cap. It was an annoying way to start something new. Nick managed to produce a few slices of bread and butter for me but I was still hungry.

I was told to go on watch at noon, the twelve to four. Lieutenant Good, the acting Captain, spent some time showing me various landmarks as we neared the Daunt Light-ship, and then he said, 'Your course is West,' leaving the Bridge. 'Send for me if you see anything.' West. I checked it on the chart and west it was. Somehow it seemed a bald and uninteresting course for one's first experience in charge of a watch. If it had been West by South ¾ South or even West ¾ North it would have had more trimmings to it and seemed more attractive. But West it was and my course-line showed me that it would be West for a long time, and the seaman at the wheel was steering West. So I settled down to what French sea-writers call *le va-et-vient* and hoped that the helmsman and the look-out did not know how little I really knew. At that time one cook, two wireless operators, Nick and I, were the only men in the crew from the Marine Service proper, the others were members of the *Muirchu*'s Fishery crew who had volunteered to transfer to the Marine Service at a specially agreed rate of pay.

Ultimately we saw nothing. The ship was stopped off Galley Head and enquiries were made from the Coast Watchers. They had seen nothing. We steamed on to the Stags and met *M.1* again. Her crew swore that when we stopped every man in our one put a fishing line over the side. Certainly we were very hungry, and we caught nothing. *M.1* had no news of the troopship, nor was the wireless helpful, so we were ordered to return to the Base to complete bunkering and draw rations. That troopship was the first of the Marine Service *canards* that flapped before my eyes and quacked in my ears.

Next day we completed bunkering and came up to the anchorage. Ashore that afternoon I heard that *M.3* was on her way and was due at five o'clock, and as I had spent a week-end some time ago at Bob Good's house I telephoned the news to his parents, who were glad to hear it because the English Channel was a lively place and she was coming from London.

But that evening I was joined by Nick with the bad news that *M.3* had been bombed in the Channel and was lost. What could I do? I could not face ringing up again, better let the news come officially. We met more and more of the crowd and sat around talking about the *M.3* fellows that we had liked so much and known such a short time. The party became something like a wake and when Nick and I returned on board we talked a lot more about it for a long time. We felt awful. We told the Watch to call us if by any chance *M.3* … but it was too much to hope for. Then I remembered a little rum I had in a flask and Nick remembered a little gin he had somewhere else so we mixed the two and turned in right away.

M.3 did arrive next day, at 5.a.m – just twelve hours later than the first story had put it – but the Watch were unable to rouse us. She had been bombed, too, but they were 'wides'.

Our next patrol set us on our regular beat, the Old Head of Kinsale to Loop Head at the mouth of the Shannon. I was still without a uniform but shared a bridge-coat with Nick as we were in separate watches. After this Lieutenant F.A. White, our regular commanding officer, rejoined us.

On the morning of his return we hove up and proceeded at about ten o'clock, or rather, at ten o'clock to the split second. Absolute punctuality was a feature of his command and 'Steam for ten' meant that at ten o'clock and not one second later he stamped on to the Bridge and rang Stand-By. As it was ten o'clock there were still two hours of my watch to go, so as soon as I had finished with the Port Control flags, which authorised us to proceed under the guns of the forts, I went back to the Bridge and hung about near the man at the wheel, eager yet respectful, retiring but ready-aye-ready – it seemed to be the perfect attitude for a Chief P.O. in the presence of two officers, one of whom he had not yet seen. I concentrated on the back of a tall and spare figure snapping out alterations of course as we passed the buoys.

'Where's your uniform?' cracked out the tall and spare figure, in the middle of his orders.

'None issued yet, sir.'

Lt Flynn, commanding M.T.B. *M.3*, Lt Fred White commanding *Muirchu* and David Rankin, Chief Engineer. Note Rankin is wearing Department of Agriculture and Fisheries uniform.

'Hmm. Port more.' He did not speak to me again until we had cleared Roche's Point.

'Set a course to the Daunt Buoy.' I fell to it. Join the Point to the Buoy, allowing for our distance off, work the rulers to the compass rose. Magnetic so-and-so, correcting it to 1940. Deviation, deviation, where's the deviation book? Deviation three degrees West. Course, S.W. by W ¼ W.

'South West by West a quarter West, sir.' No bother at all. Lieutenant White bent over the chart for an instant.

'I said the Daunt *Buoy*,' he said, 'not the Daunt Lightship.' I was facing extremely angry-looking eyes. No bother at all!

I saw those eyes glaring at me many a time afterwards, especially when I was standing by aft, trying to learn his signals for bringing the ship alongside or away from a quay.

That afternoon a cap was sent to me with orders that it was to be worn. A Fisheries cap, and too small for me, but I suppose it helped to regularise things.

I went on watch again at eight in the evening and Lieutenant White came up on the Bridge shortly afterwards. He walked up and down rapidly.

'If your course was 274 degrees,' he said, suddenly, 'eleven degrees of Easterly variation, Deviation five degrees West, how would you steer?'

Oh, Capt O.M. Wetts Ltd, stand by your pupil now! I gripped the rail of the Bridge, thought hard and told him.

He came back at once with Ship's head South East by East, Deviation four degrees West, Variation fifteen degrees West, what's your True Course? I told him. He gave me a whole row of those to do in my head and kept pacing up and down all the time. Then I thought he had finished, but I was mistaken.

'Sun's True Bearing One-sixty-two degrees, Observed Bearing one-fifty-four degrees, Variation ten degrees West, what's your Deviation?' I told him that one too. All this was flung at me over his shoulder. In bad weather I always had to keep my ears wide open and even then I sometimes had to ask him to repeat his orders, and so had the helmsmen.

Now we were on to Lights, now Tides, now back to compass.

'You see a white, a Green and a Red light dead ahead and a Red light on your Starboard bow, what are you going to do?'

Not very hard, but not very nice, without models or paper, for the beginner. I'm sure the Bridge look-out was enjoying himself if he could hear us.

'Go below and have a smoke if you like. Come back in fifteen minutes.' I moved away.

'What's your Course?' he asked sharply.

'West a half North, sir.'

'Did you expect me to guess it?' There seemed to be no answer to that one so

I went below. Nick had now left us and gone to the embryo Torpedo Shop so I had no one to tell what had been going on. When I came back to the Bridge Lieutenant White was bending over the chart under the shaded light in the wing.

'What are these?' he pointed to the Small Corrections.

'What's this … that?' he was at it again.

'Hmm! You seem to know *something* about it, anyhow. I've had your gear shifted amidships. Sign the Night Order Book. Have me called if you need me … she's all yours.' He turned on his heel and left the Bridge.

She was all mine! So something *had* come out those months of hour-out Coast Watching hour-in studying on Wicklow Head. Those evenings with Tait's or Nicholl's had not been a waste of time, as I often feared they were. Even those little crumbs of learning picked up before I joined the Service were proving useful.

We were just passing Mizen Head, rolling in the uneasy swell that is always there. I got a fix from the Fastnet and the Roancarrig and it worked out all right. I put her on her next course and the Bull came up docilely, fine on the Starboard bow.

She was all mine!

I did not notice the rest of that watch passing. At one bell before midnight I entered up the log and at midnight Lieutenant Colvin came on the bridge and my watch was over.

I remember going into the forecastle for some reason that night, as I came off watch. Everyone was asleep and I was suddenly struck by the thought that while they slept I had held their safety in my hands. There were no outlying dangers and we were well off the land anyhow, but I did not think of that just then, what I thought was … reverse the positions and you wouldn't have slept a wink.

I went below to my new quarters and into the Saloon for a cup of tea which was waiting for me there. Facing me in the half-light I saw someone with a peaked cap and a white scarf – an officer who had come aboard while I was busy at Cobh? No, myself in a mirror.

I turned in. She's all yours, he'd said, and left her to me. How long until I came on watch again?

But I got over that kind of thing quite soon, I began to realise that so far I was only touching the outside of what I had to know; increase of experience showed me how much still lay ahead. The words à Kempis were often in my mind:

Then be not raised on high in pride
For any skill or knowledge of your own
But rather fear for what has been
Entrusted to you.

Irish troops boarding the War Department vessel to take over Spike Island, 1938. The destroyer HMS *Acasta* is preparing to depart, the last British naval ship in Irish waters.

Norris Davidson, Evie Hone, 1938. Mixed media on card.

Norris Davidson in later life.

The ruin of a wartime Coast Watching Service Lookout Post.

Fitzpatrick's Guesthouse as it appears today.

CAR ASCEAĊ INS NA h-ÓŠLAIŠ

A recruitment poster for the Volunteers, the part-time army reserve of the 1930s.

Wicklow Head today. The wartime lookout post is the small building on the crest, now a radio communications facility.

1940

An aerial view of Haulbowline, 1940.

Engineer Billy Richardson, Commander George Crosby, commanding the Marine
Service Depot, and unknown.

James Morris/Seamus O'Muiris as Lieutenant Commander Royal Navy and Commander Marine Service. He was director of the Service.

A coloured drawing by Tony Inglis of Motor Torpedo Boat *M.1*. Tony was a draughtsman in the Marine Service for a short while.

SS *Shark*, the small cargo steamer of the Marine Service used for laying defensive mines in the main harbours.

Torpedoes were the principal weapon of the Marine Service.

Marine Service and Maritime Inscription on parade in Cork.

The dramatic coast of Donegal.

Killybegs some years ago, not much different to the town described by Norris.

Remote Tory Island.

Serene Lough Swilly.

The legacy. *LÉ Eithne* rescuing migrants in the Mediterranean in 2015.

7

Sighted P/V *Muirchu*

When I come to write this I realise that after five years' service in her, with some interruptions, the *Muirchu* has become my home. In her I am as independent as a tortoise carrying its shell around, and often as inert.

Long ago for me except in very bad weather, she ceased to be a small metal box capable of motion and set in the wastes of the sea. She is the place where I have my being and I have ceased to be particularly conscious of the surrounding water. A house-dweller is not continually conscious of walls, nor does he look out of the window and note that he is surrounded by ground – he just accepts it, unless he comments on its green-ness or bareness or dampness. So I accept the sea except when the weather forces its appearance on me. When I am ashore I am always conscious of being 'not on board' – not at home, but when I return I never feel 'now you are not ashore'.

Yet at the back of all this is a feeling that one is not here forever, often brought on by coming across something that a man did or made or wrote or had put on board many years ago. He probably felt himself as much a part of her as I feel myself to be, but where is he now? Where will the ship herself be when the years have rolled on? Owing largely to the matrimonial influences in the Co. Cork air, more than half the *Muirchu*'s crew have homes ashore. Many of the others on board are Depot attachments. Naturally all are on board when we go to sea but when we are anchored at the Base and the locally married men troop ashore in the evening I feel that I share the ship with only one other man, the Petty-Officer Boatswain. He has a much larger share of her because I have only five years to his twenty-six. Unlike the married men and the attachments, both of us have vast stores of momentarily useless objects which always turn in handy for something, particularly the Boatswain. In fact what the Boatswain has is beyond human knowledge. He provided a complete set of Rule of the Road models out of odds and ends, he can make toys with professional skill and an enquiry such as, 'Have you anything that would do for fixing on to this,

Bo'se,' involves immense rooting and rummaging and the inevitable finding of the next-best thing, usually a very close next best.

'That's been in her since the last War, and it's not on the Ledger.'

All her fittings and stores are carried on the Ledger. At one time in the past these stores were indented for through the Post Office, one of the strange relationships in Government services, and holystone was required for scouring the decks. The Boatswain tells a story that this caused consternation among the Postal officials. What on earth was holystone, a medicine or some magic talisman against evil at sea? No one knew, and at last they remembered that among the post office workers was an old sailor. He was summoned, a gnarled and stooped old man.

'Holystone! Do you see this hump on me back? I got that from thirty years of bloody holystone.'

123137 Muirchu (formerly the Helga) International Code Signal E. I. B. W. Port and Year of Registry, Dublin 1908. Port and year of Registry, Dublin 1908. Steel-built. 155. 6. length. 24.6. Breadth. 12.6. Depth of hold. Nett Registered Tonnage III. Gross Registered Tonnage 323. Horsepower of engines, 140.

That is how she appears in the Mercantile Navy List. She was built in Dublin as a Fishery Protection vessel, not as a yacht as her graceful lines make many people think, and she carried out her work of protection and Fishery research until the last War. Her accommodation was divided up into Forecastle, Quarters amidships for the Captain and for the scientists when they made research cruises, and quarters aft for her officers. During the last war she became H.M. Yacht '*Helga*' and patrolled the Irish Sea, sinking a German submarine by depth-charges, for which deed she still carries two stars on her funnel.

It has often been said that she shelled Liberty Hall in the Rising of 1916 and only, I think, in R.M. Fox's book *The Citizen Army* are the true facts stated. She did fire a couple of rounds at Boland's Mills under the impression that she was being shelled from there (it was actually mis-directed British Artillery fire). To bring fire to bear on Liberty Hall she would either have had to lob shells over the intervening railway bridge, for which she was too close, or to fire under the bridge, and that was too risky.

When we were open for exhibition during the Military Tattoo in 1945 I grew hoarse giving this explanation to visitors and letting them elevate and depress a gun so as to see for themselves.

After the war she resumed her Fishery work and we have on board crew-books containing the names of men, and comments upon men, who are of importance in our shipping to-day.

During the Civil War she gained an evil reputation in the ports for bringing prisoners round the coast when communications were interrupted, and for landing Free State troops at the capture of Youghal. This may have been the reason for the changing of her name to *Muirchu* from *Helga*. She was really *Helga the Second*, the first was a yacht used for Fishery work, and there was also *Changsa*, a house-boat on the Shannon, some of whose cutlery is still in use in *Muirchu*'s Wardroom Mess.

1939 saw her again on active service, re-armed and commissioned as the first Patrol-vessel of the new Marine Service, the P/V *Fort Rannoch* was also commissioned at this time. Thus she passed under army control, retaining most of her crew under a special agreement and increasing it with Marine Service recruits. A soldier-cook arrived on board in Dun Laoghaire. He came from the Artillery, wore spurs before he got his seamen's uniform and was a veteran of the Bass War. Does anyone recall that campaign?

One thing that many a visitor on board during the Tattoo learned was the stupidity of the 'The *Muirchu*, ha! … the "Irish Navy" begod' attitude of the Man in the Pub. One heard nothing but praises for the ship and whichever Flotilla happened to be alongside with her. The comic papers, pantomime jokes and the apparently screamingly funny fact of her 'one-ness' – of her being our single Government ship for so long – have fostered a giggling attitude.

'The *Muirchu*, ha! Ha! – the "Irish Navy" begod!' I would like to have some of those facetious ones on board us during a mine-sinking patrol in fogey weather, or on the Western Patrol in all winter weathers when the order was

The Marine Service exhibition in the RDS, Dublin, as part of the 1945 Military Tattoo.

'Go out, and stay out'. That would have cut short some of the 'ha! Ha's!' As for the Irish Navy ... surely after more than twenty years of comparative independence our Irishry might be implicit, and we never did more than call ourselves a Marine Service. We are a small service, we worked quietly and without audiences, we carried out our duties and in doing so some of our men lost their lives, as surely in the interests of our country, as if we had been at war.

Apart from all that, to laugh at a man's ship – even if it is only a harbour-dredger – is to show oneself as being dismally bogged down in the earth. The owner of the smallest craft will tell you the same, if he has any pride in her. He may own a little yacht or even only a sailing dinghy and when he sees an ocean racer or a large cruising yacht he will admire her – covet her, even, but he will still feel that in some way his own craft has for him something that the other man's does not and cannot have.

All right, then; she's the Boatswain's home, she's my home, she's the part-property and part-existence of everyone aboard her. She's thirty-seven years old, she's not as fast as she was and she rolls abominably but for us – she lives.

Muirchu was built in 1908 and the lovely flare of her bows and her graceful lines suggest that the great sailing ships were in her designer's mind. I know her from every angle and apart perhaps from out on her quarters or from right astern she is harmonious and a thing of the sea, born for the sea out of a great tradition. Seen from the positions mentioned the 'cabs' on her bridge make her look a little clumsy and the tallness of her silly old funnel needlessly betrays her age. I say needlessly because other vessels of her age have managed to avoid this. I have often asked the Engineers whether cutting down her funnel to the band and increasing her forced-draught would impair the efficiency of her engines, but they either just looked important or said she would cover the deck with smuts. Well, if the coal isn't good she does that anyhow with a following wind, and many a cap-cover or canvas dodger she has blackened. But maybe such an attempt at rejuvenation would be un-becoming to her age, like a face-lifting for a face that will soon be dust anyhow. Anyhow, I do not look at her from dead astern or from out on her quarter, like any other faithful lover, I close my eyes to blemishes. If I cross her bows in the launch I look up at the eyes of her, and her knife-like stem – no wonder she rolls – and at her graceful deck-line. She has two Forecastles now, the original one for the greasers and Firemen and another one built in her forehold for the Seamen. Leading-seamen, Petty Officers and C.P.O.s sleep aft. The officers are amidships and, except for the Captain and the Chief Engineer, their rooms are on the waterline, so is the saloon. The view from a boat alongside of people eating beneath one, seen through a port on the waterline, looks like a sort of submarine exhibition.

No ship is without her characters, and the *Muirchu* has had her full comple-ment of them in the short time I have been on board. The greatest I knew was her Chief Steward, James Longmore, who died in 1945 after thirty-seven years of service in her under the Department of Agriculture and Fisheries, the British Admiralty and finally the Marine Service.

Our tradition was that Longmore had been fixed in position just after her keel was laid down and that the *Helga* had then been built around him. He was at sea all his life, as a boy in the Dublin Bay pilot-boats, then in the Irish Lights, then the Fisheries. When the ship was taken over during the last War he was given the rating of C.P.O. Steward but under the Marine Service he was Seaman Longmore. From being the Captain's personal steward he became cook-steward to a Mess consisting of the Captain, a sub-lieutenant, a Sub-lieutenant Engineer and a Warrant-Officer. Like the other Fisheries men he retained his Fisheries rate of pay, which was higher than that of the Service, and it was not the additional duties, but the rating, which irked him. Unfortunately the army could not alter our Establishment and promoting Longmore to C.P.O. would have meant, in their eyes, that a Company-Sergeant Cook was looking after a Mess of four, and no Defence Force Regulation covered such a situation. They granted that his case was exceptional, but would the cook-steward for the Officers' Mess in another ship see it in that light? Wind or weather never upset him and he was on his feet from early morning until very late at night, except for a mysterious disappearance in the afternoon which he called his 'Holy Hour'. Very occasionally he would go ashore. At the end of one hot summer day we anchored off Schull and, feeling a little tired and in need of refreshment, he handed his assistant a pint bottle and a shilling and said, 'Get that filled with holy water for me and send it off under the stores you're buying.'

Later in the evening the stores were delivered and with them the bottle, wrapped in paper. James took a glass from his pantry, set off for his quarters whistling quietly, sat down for his well-earned refreshment and poured out a glass of exactly what he had ordered. The literal-minded Seaman-steward had spent a considerable time in scooping water out of the font into the bottle and had put the shilling into the Church box. When he left us we made him a presentation and with it went an album in which everyone available who had ever had anything to do with him wrote something about him; it was a sort of epitome of his service, it contained poems, sketches, and even a Guinness label neatly altered to read 'holy water'.

I'd give two thousand pounds if I was able
once more to hear your 'Gents, it's on the table'

was the lament of one gourmet. He was a great cook and a great steward, he knew his business thoroughly and anyone who has been to sea will understand all that that means. He could make a meal out of nothing and he had his special curries, his 'Hitler blanc-mange' – a sort of hamburger, his Mock Crab and his Bachelor's Omelette. When he left us someone sadly complained, 'Now-a-days a single egg is nothing more than Eggs,1.'

His galley is no longer sibilant to his eternal whistling, nor ringing to his rendering of 'The Castle of Dromore', though other songs are sung there. I think it is Dr Ommaney who comments in one of his books on the endless singing of sea-cooks. If it is any criterion of their qualities we must have two masters in Seamen Jimmy Wall, who often sings Mozart picked up from my gramophone, and in Seaman Robert Murphy, who can make the pots rattle to his hill-billies while he prepares his chef d'oeuvre, a feathery jam *soufflé,* which he makes when he can get what he calls 'civvy' eggs.

For the second greatest character I must return to Petty-Officer McKeone, the Boatswain. My first day on board I saw him eyeing me like a male statue of Justice with the scales in one hand and the bandage slightly pushed up. Long afterwards I heard him say, 'Well, I've had sharks' heads, Lancia lorries and dead men aboard this one, but what we have to-day beats everything.' I wonder if that was running through his head when he looked at the latest thing the Marine Service had thrown up. He lives in a small room at the back of a workshop which opens off the Quarterdeck and I often drop in there, if I have been ashore in the evening, to discuss the latest Depot buzz or to talk about the present situation in Fur and Feather Land, for we are both Count Curly fans. His information covers most sea-faring matters, from the British Navy, in which he served in the last War, to the depth of water on a bar, the ways of French fishermen and the family history's [sic] and behaviour of the inhabitants of many a port. Apart from the ship, his home is in Dun Laoghaire. It would be hard to say whether his home ashore or the ship is nearest his heart but, I think, stronger calls than either of these establishments are made by any dogs which happen to be around. When I joined the ship he had charge of the famous Balbo, Darkie his son and, at times, Nigger – all cocker spaniels.

Balbo was what in earlier days would have been called a chartered libertine, possibly even a licensed voluptuary, and there are many of his descendants round the coast. Certainly he knew exactly where he wanted to go whenever he went ashore, and in his extreme old age he became quite uninhibited about publicity, he even chose the august Head Post Office of a town for a place inside which to display his enterprise. He also had a habit of bringing his mistresses alongside the ship and performing before an audience. In dry-dock in Dublin with inches of snow on the ground, he would disappear, and his return to the edge of the dock with some draggled slut from the East Road always made the workmen down tools to watch the show. Sometimes he would absent himself for days in the pursuit of love and swim off to the ship if he could see no boat to take him there. Darkie, who was born at sea, was a prude and did not approve of his Father's ways at all, frequently attacking him at indelicate moments. He was McKeone's favourite but he was Longmore's enemy. Balbo, who was really a courtly old scoundrel, seldom visited the officers' Quarters, but Darkie went there at any moment he chose and would leave little pools below the panelling or against any attractive stanchion. It was worth spilling a little water near the Fore Cabin to hear Longmore's furious 'that bloody dog again!'

Nigger joined another ship, poor Darkie fell down a hold and had to be destroyed – he predeceased his father, who is buried at Alexandre Basin and has a tombstone. He had obituaries in the Dublin papers. Dogs still come and go but I don't think Petty-Officer McKeone buys sausages for them as he used to do for Darkie. At present there is a wire-haired terrier bitch on board and I hear him telling her affectionately that she is a 'Decent, respectable girl', but she is far from being that, as Mr Power's dog (another passenger) could tell, when he seized his opportunity while the crew were at their stations for anchoring.

Longmore and McKeone, I have only given you two names out of all that passed through her in my five years. I would like to give all the names, to show my regard for them, but that would scarcely interest you. Still, I am picking a few at random from the crew-list. C.P.O. Con MacCarthy, the big engineer with the 26lb. cannon-ball, and his quiet mate P.O. Donal Long. C.P.O. Lotti, who has the Gift of Figures and who unites with me whenever it appears that any authority is doing what is called 'coming the hound'. O'Sullivan and O'Regan, the wireless operators; Logue and Byrne the Leading Seamen; L/S Martin Costello and his opposite number Seaman Connell, who would fill a book with his doings; his classic remark is, 'Well, anyhow we'll never go out of this world alive.'

Seaman George Hesse, who would expect to hear brasses polished to 'Where e'er you Walk'? – but Hesse is a Feis Ceoil medallist. Seaman Peader Somers, a quiet and agreeable seaman who, in the ring, is transformed out of recognition into a formidable fighting machine and who has published some excellent short stories about the Service. Yes, this is becoming a Crew-list: White, Gannon, '22 and '13 Doyle, Waldron, Byrne, Dunne, Delton, Bowers – that is just a few of them but they are as important to the ship as her engines. Each name means a train of facts for me, Home, Rating, Mess, Action Station, Boat Station, Division, history, disposition and nick-name. I can recognise their footsteps on the deck overhead.

These men give the ship life and, in turn, they become part of her history. I resent any of them being transferred out of her, in fact I resent any change in her at all because I have probably been too long on board. But they will surely go some day, and I will surely go, and we will be just names in the Crew Book and our work will just be something that a man did or made or wrote or had put on board long ago; but not so very long ago because progress is too fast for her and in time she must go herself, with all her history and with all her memories of the lads who served in her, and with her silly old funnel. But we will remember her as we remember all lovely things and only those bogged down in the earth will not understand us.

8

Made Fast at Marine Service Depot

In spring 1941, after a spell in dry-dock, we steamed into Cobh from Dublin and met Heinkels and Dorniers on the way, so my diary tells me. After a few days we went off again on the continuous patrol and one of these included a visit to the Aran Islands, not my first since I left in 1939 but my first by sea. I recall that we went ashore through a blustery night and I went up to Mr Daly's public-house to meet anyone who might be there, but we did not stay long because the weather was getting worse, in fact that patrol was a continuous record of bad weather.

On our return we bunkered again and during this I fell down the manhole over one of the side-pockets. At one moment I was walking up the starboard alley-way, next I was in the manhole, like a very loose cork in a bottle, with my right shin spouting blood on the coal below. Fortunately it was not heaped high enough to break my leg. I remember a stoker asking me if I was all right and I testily told him to attend to his work. He hauled me out firmly. The incident caused great amusement to everyone save me.

On the day this undignified accident occurred I had received orders to report to the Depot and so I took up a purely military life except for work in the Torpedo Shop. During this time we moved into the fine new billets which had been built at the West of Haulbowline and I shared a room with Chief P.O. Alsop and Chief P.O. Dermot Murphy, who held a 2nd mate's ticket and, at the moment of writing is in Irish Shipping Ltd.

I had already done several brief courses in the Torpedo Shop at times when the *Muirchu* was in, this was my first thorough one and Mr Power laid in to us with all he had, and that was plenty. Nick Kennedy was already his unof-

Marine Service personnel parading. By 1941 the Service had settled into disciplined organisation.

ficial second-in-command and knew torpedoes thoroughly from hard work, intensive reading and bold secret experiments. I know that twenty-two years are supposed to go in the making of a torpedo-man, but I doubt it.

We now had our own compressor for the air-bottles, a terrifying piece of machinery when I compare it with the compact installation in the new torpedo-shop. When it was first started up all of us found it convenient to go outside for as long as possible to avoid being blown up with it.

This course took us up from the beginning again. I recall the 'waiting-pressure' of air in some niggling little valve in the gyroscope, the Main Reducer and its 'dashpot', the Hydrostatic valve, the Timing Gear and the Greenock Depth and Distance gear, which Mr Power told us not to interfere with, so we opened it. There was, too, the maddening job of adjusting rudders 'with and without air'. If you were prepared to sit down and suck up knowledge unquestioningly you learned a lot, but if you went the least bit off your course with a, 'Well, why doesn't the increase of Back Pressure etc. etc.,' Mr. Power would say stuffily. 'All right, go ahead. Invent your own torpedo and bring us the plans. I'm sure we'll all be very interested.' The fact was that we had to learn the essentials as quickly as possible.

'That's the summary of that lot going through there,' Mr Power would snap, as he passed on to the next component. Then we came to the stripping and assembly of torpedo-engines. The engine itself was simple enough, the stripping and assembly was *wording* awful. The worst part of it was the removal and replacement of six copper pipes, two of them double-ended and four of them with three ends. I kept a note book by me and, with oily fingers, entered each operation in the stripping before putting the part removed into an oil-bath. As the pipes were the hardest part of it I nicked each one of them with strokes from one to six as they came off. My note-book then told me how each numbered Pipe should go back, but I was observed. Kennedy nicked every one of my pipes up to six and left me to guess which was which. In my fair copy of those greasy notes I read the inspiring message:

11. Remove the Brotherhood Ring. Note that it is Dished to prevent wrong replacement.

Those Brotherhood Rings – they sounded like the insignia of a secret order – kept us guessing for two days while Mr. Power sat on a work-bench swinging his legs and mocking at our hopes of ever becoming torpedomen.

The notes continue:

12. With long screw-driver ease out the Crank Pin Bush.

I suppose I knew what I meant then, I certainly don't now.

We were really working backwards, we held our ratings but we were being educated up to them. We could manage to stagger through our other duties and now we had to be crammed with torpedo-knowledge. At the end of our first stripping and assembly two C.P.O.s reported their engine ready for a run with air on. They were told to make a last search round to see if any washers had been forgotten in the oil-bath, and there they found a piston.

Chief Petty Officers and Petty Officers took turns at doing Duty Petty Officer in the Depot, attending the Officer of the Day at Flag Down and preparing the Guard for Guard Mounting. He spent the night in the Telephone Switch Room, and visiting sentries. During one of these nights I wrote lines to memorise the thirty-two Torpedo Preparation Tests on which we were working. I think it's out of date now. It held such frantic advices as:

When for adjustment she is upside-downed
Don't turn on air until the bastard's round.

and

But keep the clamps on or, I swear, this hour
Will be your last, beware of Mr Power!

and ended

> Learn this by heart, you'll gain your greatest wish
> And underneath your stripes wear crossed tin-fish.

But we never did. We qualified all right and various insignia were issued but the torpedoman's was crudely made and was not approved.

When we weren't in the Torpedo Shop we were working on torpedo tubes and firing gear aboard the M.T.B.s. My diary says,

> Monday. 26th May 1941. M.3's Port side-stop not engaging

and, very honestly,

> Tuesday. 27th May. Worked in M.3 in the forenoon. Broke her
> Starboard Teleflex and bent a Depth Charge pistol in the Afternoon.

That was one way of getting to know *M.3*'s gear.

An elderly seaman who used to work in the Torpedo shop at this time hated C.P.O.s – 'The only difference between me and that *worder* is that he has three *wording* stripes on his arm, and *word* that for difference.' In many ways he was correct.

Suddenly he became pregnant with rumour and sidled up to each one of us confidentially.

'I hear some of the Chief P.O.s are going to get a great suck-in,' he would hiss maliciously. 'There's some *wording* big Test coming off and some of the Chief P.O.s are going to walk the plank – of course I don't mean yourself, Chiefie,' he would add hastily. For once, the buzz was true. There was going to be a Navigation and Seamanship test for C.P.O.s in addition to a torpedo-test, and when we fell out for a smoke in the Torpedo Shop we turned to knots and splices. Unwilling, yet with a sort of fascinated horror, this seaman would sidle up to us.

'No! – No! That's not right, Chief,' he would snarl, pointing at a tangle of ropes.

'He's doing it wrong – he's doing it wrong – look at him,' he would appeal to us, 'he's doing it *wording* wrong.' Then he would remain quite for a little, but shaking with rage. 'Give it to me, sir,' would eventually come from between his clenched teeth.

'Give it to me!'

'Give it to me, Chief!' And then his patience would go.

'Give me the *wording* thing!' and with few twists of his hands he would set it right.

He was an interesting character, disliking us and yet never keeping away from us when we were in the Torpedo Shop. He told us once how he had sat for his mate's ticket and had been put out by the examiner because he prompted the other candidates. From this picturesque tale we decided that he had probably failed for a life-boat or E.D.H. certificate. One of the questions in this interesting examination was, 'What would you *wording* do if you broke the green glass in your Starboard light?' We gathered round.

'Use an oil light.'

'Naw!'

'But you would ... you'd use an oil light.'

'Naw, that doesn't matter, it's not the answer.'

'Ship a spare glass, then?'

'Naw!' he sneered at us. We gave it deeper thought.

'Put green paint on plain glass or on the bulb – use green bunting.'

'Naw, sir, naw! That's not the answer.'

'What is the answer, then?'

'Use blue glass.'

'Blue glass? But where would you get it?'

'You'd *wording* have it.'

'But where would you have it, what use would it be?'

'You'd *have* it, you'd *have* to have it!'

'Did you ever see blue glass in a ship?'

'Naw!'

'Then why would you have to have it on board?'

'Because it's the answer.' Nothing would shake him. 'If you went to the examiner and said anything else you wouldn't be put out of the room, you'd be *worded* out.'

For some reason this examination was voluntary, apart from the torpedo part. When this was announced many who thought they would be compelled to sit dropped out 'as a matter of principle'. It was a great caller of bluffs. Some of our army instructors who were being transferred into the Marine Service studied hard and sat for the examination but without any sensational success, which was surprising considering that they managed to get hold of the papers the night before.

The only advantage that I saw in life in the Depot was the increased freedom to go ashore. In the patrol-vessels we placed enormous value on a week-end, or even a day, ashore. Looking back now from our safety it may seem a little foolish but we could never be absolutely sure that each departure might not be our last. Plenty of shipping was being lost round our coasts, might it be our turn next? We were only few miles away when the *Kerry Head* simply disappeared, no one knew what happened to her. [She was attacked twice. The second time was in sight of watchers in Cape Clear island and she sank with all hands. Ed.] Hardly a watch passed without wreckage being sighted, and then there were the various alarms and stand-tos. The earliest big one of these was on the 20th December 1940. The *Muirchu* was at the Deepwater Quay and I was in the Depot on various errands. Suddenly I was detailed to go with some others and help to bring an off-duty M.T.B.'s torpedoes into the First Degree of Readiness, after loading them on board. What was on now? And the ball was hopping: the *Scharnhorst* or the *Hood* was expected off Roches Point at 3 p.m. The alternatives and the precise time were interesting and we thought that if they both managed to keep the appointment their attentions might be diverted from us.

'Well,' said an engineer of rather imperialist sympathies, 'I hope it isn't the *Hood*, I might be firing on friends of mine.'

'You won't be asked to,' said an unidentified voice in the busy crowd, 'you'll be down in the engine-room if you're doing your job.' And we still don't know who made that very sensible comment.

Then a launch took me off to the *Muirchu* and we resumed patrol at once, with only two days' rations on board because we had expected to be in for some days longer.

Our Christmas dinner was grand, bully beef and ship's biscuits at sea off Kerry. I came on deck after this feast just in time to sing out, 'Aircraft to port!' and Action Stations followed. But it was one of our bombers on patrol. Shortly after that we got a radio from the Minister for Defence wishing us a Happy Christmas, it was kind of him, but we couldn't eat it.

By coincidence I am typing this from my manuscript on Christmas Eve 1945 and we are weather-bound off the coast of Wexford. This time we have the rations, and, I suppose, we will have the Christmas wishes as well.

The days were tense because we did not know when invasion was coming. We knew that all we could do would be, in a very small way, to act the part of the coat which it is said to be advisable to throw to a pursuing bull in order to delay him. After that it was up to the soldiers. One thing we were certain of was that invasion *would* come. At the end of official summer in 1940 some of us were taking off our white cap-covers and wondering if we would put them on next May, and this wasn't being morbid it was just the normal feeling at the time. After the event it may seem silly but so do most things after the event.

So the Depot was a complete change from all this. On board we were a small ship's-company and everyone knew pretty well what everyone else would feel, think or do in a large number of different circumstances but in the Depot I had a wide choice of companionship, from my serious room-mates, who were deeply busy writing to their respective dames, to the society of the completely irresponsible. It was an opportunity for looking round and seeing how things stood with the others whom I had not regularly seen since our early days in Collins Barracks and Spike Island.

Recreation was, and still is, badly neglected – especially for the men; and I speak with experience of military barracks too. What way of passing the time has a sailor or soldier who is, perhaps, sending home a few shillings a week, paying off a railway-warrant or a deduction for kit and trying to have a few cigarettes each day? I knew of one sailor who, all honour to him, regularly sent home eighteen shillings out of his pay of one pound and two-pence per week. After taking off the overheads I have mentioned the remaining sum may only run to a few beers or a couple of evenings at the cinema. And then what?

You can't walk round a city, or some little village outpost, forever. All hands can't play billiards simultaneously at the few tables. Put a man in his country's defence in a confined place on a winter evening and when he has read every-thing available and sung everything, and cribbed about everything, and when he doesn't want to sleep his idleness may lead him to do something foolish and he may find himself up before his Commanding Officer on a Charge. I don't want to give you a picture of ships and barracks filled with brooding idle men at the end of the week. It is a matter of temperament, some men take things philo-sophically and others do not, and in general the men had little done for them.

Here and there committees worked magnificently to entertain the soldiers posted among them, but only here and there. There is a generous cinema pro-prietor in Dublin who admits members of the Defence Forces for half-price and will continue to do so, he says, while there is a Defence Force. And there were firms which organised cinema entertainments for troops, but I read recently of a committee which sent a huge number of parcels of comforts to troops abroad and distributed a few of them to their local L.D.F. Maybe the view, of that committee was that our country was being defended abroad; maybe it was – indirectly and not entirely from motives of affection – but surely they realised that many thousands of their countrymen were under arms all around them and were prepared to defend them, regardless of what views they held? I don't think I am being small-minded when I suggest that Coast Watchers also felt the cold, that sailors clearing mines for ships bringing food to that Committee knew the icy nip of the east wind? However, that is all a matter of civilian enterprise. Our more immediate crib was against our own authorities. Where were the travelling cinemas visiting military posts, and our Depot, at the thin end of the week? Where were the travelling libraries? Where were the radio-grams that might have provided a concert of records selected by vote to pass dark winter evenings? Well, maybe some of the things I mention were here, maybe some of them were there, and their [sic] is a cinema in Fort Berehaven, but why are not these things general? For the Marine Service there was nothing except one concert party and a superb collection of books from the Carnegie Library, the administration of which, I am sorry to say, was hopelessly mismanaged.

On board the *Muirchu*, in spite of many applications, we have only been given three packs of cards and a ring-board in five years. A wireless-set with loudspeakers in the four Messes would cheer up this sad Christmas Eve on Mine Patrol. Application for it was turned down long ago.

I don't believe that unwillingness is the fault, it is thoughtlessness and it is this unimaginative neglect that is often talked over in ships and barrack rooms. Memories of good times and bad times grow dim in the end but memories of prolonged stretches of boredom leave something behind which influenced many men when, in 1945, they decided not to prolong their service.

As it was early summer-time when I went into the Depot I began to think of rowing. Not rowing in light fours or eights because the Harbour was much too exposed for continuous training, though these craft, which are known locally as Gigs, have competed in Harbour Regattas. The Harbour racing craft were First Class Salmon Yawls, Whalers and Pleasure Boats. For me a Pleasure Boat had meant a sort of tub-four with a garden-seat arrangement for the coxswain, and I think the Cork craft developed out of this original into a rather beamy 28-foot boat with fixed pins and fixed seats and no outriggers. Many of them were built at Oxford, or on the Thames.

Blackrock Rowing Club were kind enough to lend us a boat (which we subsequently bought) and this part of the Marine Service Rowing was turned over to me. Time was short and it was hard to collect a crew but I eventually settled down to four men, Seamen (Now P.O.) Thuillier, Seamen White, Seamen Wilshaw and, Stroke, Seamen O'Mahony [sic]. For about a fortnight I coxed myself, suffering awful cramps, and then, when the crew were beginning to get together and she was running evenly, I handed the boat over to John Cashin, the man whom I had picked out in Collins Barracks a year before. He then weighed a shade under eight stone and he got a complete control of his crew even when he was only learning to steer. I soon saw that these craft did not 'carry their way' at all and that rowing them required an 'in-out' style with which the smooth spring and draw of a racing eight was impossible. We did little about training. I think a moderate smoker, providing that he is an adult, is best allowed to continue smoking. This was especially so in our case because stopping smoking means increased appetites which the ration-scale could not have satisfied completely, though egg-flips were provided. Anyhow, I realised that a man living the normal and regular life of the Depot was naturally in good training, far better training than we were ever in at Cambridge before the periods of strict training started.

Our first regatta was a disaster. We entered for both Junior and Senior races at Cobh and in each of them O'Mahony, a powerful stroke, broke an oar at the start. In 1942 we had two crews and got some second prizes.

In 1943 we had two boats, though the Welfare Board refused to do more for our branch of the rowing than purchase singlets and pay part of our fares to regattas. In this year, too, we won a challenge cup at Kinsale and first prize at Cobh. We were by now, with the Commander's approval, a completely separate sports unit in the Service. Cashin became too heavy to cox and turned out to be as good as a coach as he had been in the boat.

Seaman Donnelly, a Dublin man too, was our new cox. As rowing was voluntary it was often hard to insist on a man's going out with a crew and losing part of a summer night ashore, but the officers became more and more helpful in allowing men time off their duties and so we were, in the end, able to row at almost any time of day provided that the weather was suitable; but the weather often stopped us from launching a boat for as long as a fortnight, while up-river crews could train in sheltered waters. There was every kind of annoyance attached to the rowing but this was all compensated for in the end by the excitement of the regattas, towing the boats up to the start, last-minute instructions, and then the race itself. There was Ross, a brilliant stroke, and the tireless Wilshaw, and Seaman 'Boston Burglar' Smith, and Foley and L/S Howard and Cashin – savage or pleading – driving them on to give all they had. With training in eights in a first-class club these men would have shown up well at Henley. It was a pity that regatta conditions, except at Cork, were not worthy of the men. Again and again Starters have spoken to me of the discipline and steadiness of the Service crews in remaining on the starting line and not trying to steal a few lengths ahead, even though it was always to their disadvantage. The Marine Service Rowing Club gave me, at different times, a gold medal and a clock, which was very generous of them. I consider that they did all the hard work and I got most of the fun.

But rowing was only a summer activity and the other Depot amusements seemed brief. Basket Ball did not last very long, the weekly dances fell through; Question Time had its innings and Football and Hurling seemed to follow no organised programme of training. And Rowing seemed to be the only sport whose members kept them alive, and we supported each other with a fair amount of enthusiasm. I have never enjoyed watching boxing very much but when the men belong to your own crowd it makes a difference and I followed the boxing as much as I could. From 1941 onwards we nearly always had a company of the Construction Corps with us and these lads provided a lot of impromptu concerts and boxing. I always remember one hero in the ring who, when beaten on points, said in astonishment, 'If I'd-a known I wasn't winning I'd-a *worden* him out the window.'

Though I say that much more might be done for sailors and soldiers in Barracks, I think a lot of the entertainment should develop from inside; if men have worked for a thing themselves it gives a lot of satisfaction. One most successful Depot entertainment was an entirely home-produced play by L/S Liam Smith which we toured round the harbour. This was a really good form of evening recreation. About twenty-five or thirty men were busy on it, the Supplies Stores produced the fire-arms and ammunition, the Draughtsmen painted the scenery that the Carpenters made, the Electricians lit the stage, the Orderly Room printed the programmes and the only expense was the hiring of costumes. There were weeks of pleasant work for those in the Depot who were getting that play ready.

But that was only once in a while, and a cinema (sub-standard sound projector) and a big library would help in every Barracks, Marine Service or military, without stifling internal enterprise.

More than anything else the food needs to be improved, and the conditions under which it is eaten. From the start the army fed us on a higher scale than the soldier, but what happens to the undoubtedly very good raw materials of meals when they arrive in the Depot or on board a patrol-vessel? The cooks are qualified cooks, that is to say they have passed through an Army School of Cookery (one does not know what the Test Piece was) but on board ship, or in the Depot they only perform the Roast, the Fry and the Boil (they are taught nothing about the technique of keeping bits of this and that back for tea or turning bones into soup for supper). [Note: Norris had 'deleted' this sentence but I've left it in as I think it is relevant, Ed.] The meal the army calls 'Tea' is not really a meal at all. For this reason many men aboard ship prefer to breakfast on bread and butter and have their breakfast rations served at four-thirty. To my mind this four-thirty meal is just as important as lunch, especially for men who will be going on night duty. The patrol-ration the army supplies for stokers doing a hefty job, for helmsmen or for Night Sentries is not nearly adequate. These army-trained sea-cooks may be instructed in how to put bits of this and that aside for tea (at the expense of the dinner-ration) and how to turn bones into soup for supper, but I never yet met one of them who do this without being told to.

Have the cooks trained by the army by all means, for the present, ours is not yet a large enough Service to support its own School, but first send the man to sea under another cook. When it is known that he will not be sea-sick and that he can keep his galley fire going and can boil water without scalding himself then let him go on a Cookery Course, but attach an old merchant-service man to each Course and both soldier and sailors will benefit greatly. Things were different in the early days in the M.T.B.s and I will come to that later.

Conditions of eating might be improved too. Why should a man voluntarily give up a comfortable home and be compelled to eat at a bare table and scour his plate before bringing it up again for whatever follows the meat or fish? Let the tables be scrubbed white in the interests of health and good appearance, but then cover them with a cloth. Let table-napkins be provided, too. There is nothing silly about this, it is simply to meet changed conditions. A men's life as a soldier or sailor is restricted by his conditions of service and there is no need to make him eat like a convict in addition. I know what I'm talking about, from a private soldier's dining-hall to the Ward-room mess in a Patrol Vessel; perhaps I bore you, but not − I think − if you, too, have faced a mug of blue tea and chopped your bread on a tin plate.

Another objection to Depot administration is that it has been a dead-end for so many men who joined the Service to go to sea and found themselves spending their years on General Duties, spending so many years in one employment that it became tacitly understood that they were Wharf-men or Ferry-Men or Mess Waiters and nothing else. Furthermore, the Depot became so like a Barracks then it was quite startling to some departments when they were reminded that the Depot existed for the ships, not the ships for the Depot. Army control is at the bottom of it, control without any malevolence on the army's part, but control of sailors by soldiers cannot imagine our necessities. Army control was most necessary at the start, just as army machinery was necessary to feed, pay and clothe us, but from the moment when the Service began to move of itself, when Seaman-writers were able to distinguish between an A.F. 295 A and an A.F. 117 and when the first Petty-Officer (not a converted soldier) was capable of giving instruction in our arms, then control should have gradually passed into the hands of the Service proper, with one Liaison Officer from the army connecting us with Dublin. A very satisfactory situation would then have come into being because the administration would have understood what it was dealing with. We were once short of two firemen in the *Muirchu* and asked for two replacements.

'Can't be spared,' said the Army, 'Shut down two furnaces.'

That epitomises our troubles, and the firemen have the hardest time of it, I think.

Can you visualise a man working in the stokehold and wearing army boots and a fatigue suit over his heavy woollen singlet? At best he may be allowed to wear a disused white flannel, but in either case he has no soap allowance. How can an army officer in charge of clothing, with the best will in the world, understand a sailor's requirements? And if he does not understand them how can he understand the engineer-Officers' demands for more suitable clothing for their men, and press for them? The supply of soap to a patrol-vessel is so fantastically small that I would not be believed if I told it. A sailor's soap-ration is not sufficient and a fireman's soap-ration is almost useless. The supply of soap in this country is small but there are cases which are 'must haves', and an officer in the Technical Stores with a knowledge of life on board ship should make demand after demand for a special supply of soap with 'must have, must have, must have' attached to it. There is a way of getting round every difficulty and the preservation of health is very important in a service. Perhaps I bore you again, but not if ingrained coal-dust has made your back come out in blisters.

The one part of the Depot with which the ships were nearly always in harmony was the Ration Stores, presided over by the ferocious Warrant-Officer Crinnion who, in spite of his language (twenty-one variants on the word *word* clocked in thirty seconds), and in spite of his having been a soldier set himself out to understand what ships needed.

Things could be greatly improved by a little consideration. Coming back off patrol we often sent a wireless message ahead asking the Depot to deliver our rations to us on arrival. But when we were anchored at the Base that evening did the Depot send off a launch with our Rations, mails and laundry? Ah, no.

In the Depot's eyes we were, I think, not a ship returning to her anchorage, a mile or so away from them, but a lorry-load of soldiers returning to an outpost. Would a barracks send out rations, mails and laundry? No, let them come in with their own lorry.

Perhaps, once more, I bore you – but not if at the end of a long day you have wanted to have a good meal and then lie down and smoke and read your mails.

9

Sighted the First Flotilla

'His name's Davidson. He was in the *Muirchu* and he's a proper bastard.' This, Jack Bellamy told me, is how their new C.P.O. was described in advance in the forecastle of M.T.B. *M.3*. I joined *M.3* in June 1941; Commanding Officer, S/Lieut J. Flynn; Engineer-Officer, Ensign Mansfield. Under Ensign Mansfield in the engine-room was Petty-Officer Bellamy (who got us to help him in turning his father's car upside down in Collins Barracks) and my Leading-Torpedoman was L/S McLaughlin (now Chief Petty Officer).

I was very happy in the M.T.B.s. They were cramped compared with my quarters in the *Muirchu* but luxurious when one thinks of what one puts up with in a small yacht, and much less cramped than the quarters in the Second Flotilla.

Abaft the chain-locker was a small wash-room with shelves which we used for sea-boots, steel helmets and respirators. The forecastle had gas-pipe cots, lockers, a collapsible table and a pressure-heater; *M.1*, which was originally designed for Esthonia [sic], actually had sort of steam-heating and various queer Esthonian words on the controls. Cut off from the forecastle was the surprisingly large galley and the quarters amidships were divided longitudinally abaft a bulkhead. To starboard was the wardroom with two folding bunks for the officers and a writing desk and wash-room. To Port were two cots for the C.P.O. and Engineer P.O. and also the wireless-room. This space was slightly larger than that of a sleeping car. Here, too, was the ship's armoury. Then came the engine-room, the petrol tanks, and the After Peak, which contained stores and ammunition and out which of all the rumours were supposed to come. The Chart-room was reached through an Action Shelter which we usually used for steering though there were duplicate controls in the chart-room, and the armament at that time consisted of rifles, a Madsen gun, Lewis Guns, depth-charges and two torpedoes.

The belly coming, as it does, a good first where matters of comfort aboard ship or anywhere else are concerned, I must begin this account of time spent in M.T.B.s by saying that except when I was directly ministered to by Longmore in the *Muirchu* I never had such good meals as I had in the M.T.B.s, nor with better appetite. The reason was simple, there was no officially trained cook. The total of the ship's company was only ten so every seaman had to cook, took turns week-about at being duty-cook, and, since his galley opened directly on the forecastle, got direct and forceful criticism of his efforts.

'What do you call this?'

'Stew.'

'Stew? … it is in my *word*.'

'Cop yourself on! Where you come from you never see stew like that from one end of the year to the other.'

'I'm *wording* sure we don't, for *word's* sake.'

'Proper order!' chime in the others.

'Stick out your hands! Try making it yourselves. I'm not a cook.'

'Damn sure you're not.'

There was no bad cooking because comment like this rather discouraged it. Except for the officers we all messed together and subscribed each week for extras, increasing by sixpences from one shilling a week for seamen up to two-and-six for C.P.O.s. My diary for Monday October 13, after a note that *M.2* still owes us two gallons of paraffin, speaks of a stew of corned beef, vermicelli, onions and grated parmesan cheese. That rococo dish was made for us by a seaman called Ronnie Curran who came from Co. Down and said he had learned it at sea from a Maltese cook, and it was provided out of our Mess funds.

In those days the Chief P.O.s in M.T.B.s were the hardest-worked men in the Service. They had to take a hand in any job they were having done on deck and, in addition, they had to assist with the various ship's books and, most important of all, see to the maintenance of the torpedoes. The routine is differ-ent now but in 1941/42 they were launched back weekly, by a tackle we called the 'Convenient William' [usually called 'Handy Billy' Ed.], and examined. Launching back was not too bad but launching in again was a job calling for all hands, including the W/T operators who – through some edict from Command – were rather untouchable. Now-a-days all this work seems to be carried out by Torpedo ratings from the Torpedo Shop but we aimed at being self-contained and Mr. Power used to come around and inspect the results.

Keeping the mahogany decks in good shape was another endless task, with scrapers, paint-remover, oil and varnish. Certainly the completed job was worth looking at for as long as it lasted but that was not long, and then the tiresome

Loading a torpedo with a 'Convenient William'.

business began again. Eventually they were painted grey, a shameful thing when one thinks of the beautiful wood but the only way of preventing it from being entirely scraped away in our efforts to keep it looking handsome.

Another feature of life was the tendency of the Depot to raid us as we lay in the basin awaiting our turn for patrol. The Depot view was that a ship off duty was filled with a crowd of idle sluggards who spent their time sleeping, and for those men there could only be one place – the Square. If we were not obviously working round the ship or on torpedoes these raids were met by well-reasoned statements of the Strength of the Ship's Company; one man Watch Below, one man in the Galley, W/T operator testing with Cork – do not disturb; Engineer P.O. and L/S and one seaman, in the engine-room doing some minor overhaul; Chief P.O. working with the Captain on the Ship's Ledger; Remains available for Training, Seamen, 1.

Of course training was necessary, especially in the maintenance of our arms, and if invasion had come the survivors of the Marine Service after its destruction would have been required to fight on land. Training won in the end and to-day the sailor in the Marine Service has to be a qualified soldier in addition to being able to carry out all his duties in the department to which he belongs. M.T.B. personnel now live in the M.T.B. Billets (except the duty M.T.B.) and eat in the Depot Messes. But necessary as this may be I am sure that the life is not nearly as good as the life we used to lead when each ship was a separate unit, though it is probably a better system for administrative purposes.

Good though the life was, nearness sometimes caused trouble. I remember walking back from the Mess one evening talking to Dick Cotter. It was dead low water and the M.T.B.s were not visible from the wall. Suddenly I heard shouts below and an L/S on the deck of *M.3* informed me frantically that murder, at least, was being done below. I went down the ladder as fast as I could, through the action-shelter, down the companion, through my quarters and into the forecastle which appeared to be filled with men fighting. I grabbed the nearest in a sort of smothering tackle but let him go when I realised that he was Seaman Ellis, the man on duty, who was trying to keep the peace. I then saw the two murderers. One was lying panting under a steel ladder leading to the deck – a little fellow, the other was clinging to a cot and breathing heavily – a huge fellow. There was blood everywhere; on their faces, their fists and their flannel vests – more serious, there was blood on my freshly enamelled bulkhead. Both heroes were completely spent. Apparently the quarrel had started late in the afternoon and actual hostilities had broken out about an hour previously. The big fellow had been finally provoked by nagging and the little fellow had made up for his size by skill. They were both seamen from the West and I seem to remember that they had been confined to ship for some small offence. I told them to wash themselves, clean up the forecastle and turn in. Dick Cotter, watching from the P.O.'s accommodation, admirably assumed the expression of a visiting Chief P.O. shocked beyond words. As no damage had been done, except to themselves, I did not bring them before the old man but contented myself with delivering a thorough 'lousing' in the morning.

During this time we did torpedo-trials on the Torpedo Range, which was down the channel. The whole point of these trials was that it was a test of a torpedo prepared by the Chief P.O. and Leading-Torpedoman of the M.T.B. concerned, not merely set for depth, range and speed, but previously stripped, assembled, fuelled and tested. And then we endured the shame of the Surface Run, the Porpoising Run and the type of run which ended with the fish bursting prematurely from the water and stopping with a derisive puff from the Holmes light. We were mostly very fortunate and, at the moment of writing, we have only lost one torpedo; we recovered one lost many years ago, and the Torpedo Shop made its engine run again too.

Our chief duty in the M.T.B.s was what we called the 'Dawn Patrol' and at this we took turns of one week each. When I joined *M.3* she was on this patrol and my first experience of steering her was taking her away from the wall and turning her in the half-light – a bit alarming since I did not know the feel of the twin rudders. I shall always remember how I burned my hands by merely easing my grip to let the wheel come amidships when the engines were running Full Ahead. The M.T.B.s of the Second Flotilla have balanced steering and this means an easier job for the coxswain. Nothing much stands out in my mind in connection with the 'Dawn Patrol' except the morning when the hydrophone slipped dumbly overboard into the vasty deep ... and our two fires.

I am prejudiced against fires at sea, particularly when they occur in the engine-room, immediately forward of about two thousand gallons of high-octane petrol. Our first fire occurred in the early morning when the E.R.A.s were changing over from running on the Main Engines to running on the auxiliaries. Extra fire extinguishers were immediately passed down the hatch and the sprinkler system was turned on with enthusiasm, causing intense discomfort to the engineers below. I went to my Fire Station down in the After Peak, with L/S McLaughlin to assist me in getting the ammunition out of the magazine and over the side if necessary.

'How about sending up the cheap stuff first, sir,' this cautious and excellent Donegal man shouted down the hatch, meaning that the .303 ammo should be thrown away first and the Madsen shells later on. That fire was quickly put out and we did not have to ditch anything. Our next fire broke out a few days later under similar circumstances but it was a rather boring little fire and one extinguisher settled its hash.

This fire business had an unexplained echo in my mind some years later. I was back in the *Muirchu*, we were lying in the Basin, and I dreamed that I was in an M.T.B. with Seamen Ellis (the peace-maker in the fight episode) and in my dream Ellis himself was on fire. I put out the flames by smothering them with my blue rain-coat, much as I had grabbed him during the actual struggle. When I woke I thought over this dream and put it down in my diary, as I sometimes do having read *An Experiment with Time*. Some hours later I was urgently called to go out in *M.4* because her C.P.O. was not available. I started to run round the Basin and then, as the weather looked threatening, I turned back, got my raincoat and made all speed to *M.4*, whose engines were running. As the tide was low I threw my raincoat to a man on deck before jumping. The man was Ellis, he had been transferred to *M.4*. As soon as I had an opportunity I told him about my dream.

'That's very strange, sir,' he said, 'just before you came on board we were talking in the forecastle about those fires.'

I didn't enjoy that trip in *M.4* one bit, not one little bit. But nothing happened. Quite a pointless little dream apparently, and quite a pointless little coincidence of a man and a raincoat. Everyone is supposed to have a story about a dream somewhere and one about a dog. I promise not to give you anything more in either line, not even about L/S Joxer, the Marine Service mascot, a courtesy-Airedale who used to go to the Greyhound Track in Cork by train every week by himself.

The result of these conflagrations was that *M.3* went out of commission for overhaul and the crew went to the Depot for Training each forenoon, sleeping there and spending the afternoons working on board. L/S McLaughlin and I remained on board as caretakers. At this time the anti-Typhoid inoculations began and caused as much alarm and discussion as the blood-grouping was to cause later on; it was impossible to convince some men after grouping that one type of blood was not an indication of a superior type of health. A friend of mine deliberately gave a sensational account of the inoculation, saying, 'I think it's quite right to have the Chaplain in the Medical Hut but it's not really necessary to have the P.A.s holding the customers down.' This invention so scared one man from Kenmare that he pretended he had been inoculated and actually walked about with a supposed sore arm tucked into his jacket until his Medical History Sheet caught him out.

Shortly after *M.3* went out of commission I moved to *M.2* under Lieutenant Austen, an ex-Blue Star officer whose heart is never very far from that line. Sparks and I had a game called 'Getting Harry down to B.A.'. The best time for playing it was just after re-fuelling.

'We could go a long way with what we've got aboard now, sir.'

'Yes.'

'How far is it to – say, the Azores, sir?' from Sparks.

A chart comes out.

'Ah, yes. The Azores – grand about this time of year,' the captain reaches for the dividers. 'Let me see – given good weather – we might run on the auxiliaries at a pinch – by God, yes, it wouldn't be bad to be down there now.'

By the rules of our game no one could mention B.A. directly.

'We could hold up some oil-wharf when we got out there and re-fuel again, sir.'

'Push on somewhere else then, sir?' says Sparks.

'Yes – I wouldn't mind seeing the old Frigorifico in B.A. sticking up. I remember one night in B.A. – I was only an apprentice at the time …' Harry is down in Buenos Aires, well on his course, nothing to do but sit back and enjoy it. Some years later when I was in the *Muirchu*, under his command, we used to go to B.A. for a little bit every day after lunch if Lieutenant Rankin, the Chief Engineer, did not take us to India or China. Indeed one afternoon we had to send for more coffee because the Chief got us firmly and entrancingly jammed in Vladivostok.

But this was only an occasional relaxation in *M.2*. There was the same torpedo routine, the same scraping, the same painting. And then the mines began.

In 1941 the mine-sinking business started to boom. The great mine-field of the allied powers had been laid from three miles off Mine Head, of all suitable names, to the English coast and the south-easterly gales were breaking them away from their moorings and causing them to drift into the path of coastal shipping, into fishing villages, under cliffs and even up rivers. We became very busy indeed.

I never knew why we were not more frequently stationed near the dangerous areas instead of having to proceed thereto from the Base. At first we expended prodigious quantities of ammunition on mines, I would not like to say how much or of what calibres. Then we realised that, except in extremely bad weather, machine-guns were not worth using on them. Rivalry began between the ships as to who sank mines with the smallest number of rounds. Eventually four riflemen took it in turn to fire five rounds each; knowing that three other men, and those on the bridge, were watching tended to increase the accuracy of each man's aim. Some mines were slow and stubborn to sink, others obligingly and appallingly exploded. I remember a seamen who came straight from the Depot to the *Muirchu* and exploded a mine with his first shot.

'I couldn't help it, sir,' he apologised in a scared voice as the roar died away and the metal fragments began to come down. Every explosion caused a considerable amount of minor damage to the ship.

One Sunday at noon we got a call to put down a mine about eight miles west of us. As we cleared Roches Point we accidentally found a mine and dealt with it before proceeding. Lieutenant Austen was now fuming with an impatience no one could understand. We found our mine right enough and it was a stubborn one, but we put it down in the end. The skipper's mood was not improved when we spotted another one. No one could understand him because he usually enjoyed these trips and sometimes took a rifle himself. Returning towards Cobh at full speed we were signalled by a yacht; a mine off Power Head. This seemed to be the last straw to our Lieutenant and when it had given up the ghost we roared away to the Deepwater Quay at Cobh instead of the Basin.

'Ring off when you've made her fast, C.P.O.,' said Lieutenant Austen, shinning up the quay ladder like lightning. And then we found the reason for his hurry; his first-born was being christened that day and because of the mines he was too late for the service. One of the best remarks I ever heard made on a mine-patrol came from Longmore in the *Muirchu* after an explosion, 'I suppose you went to break every plate in me pantry: Didn't I tell you those things were dangerous.'

When business was brisk we had not much time for shore-leave and I began to note down exactly what everyone said and did during the sinking of a mine. Then I began to work it up into a radio-documentary: I had only done one script since the one I wrote in Aran in 1939. I had no time to do more than prepare a first draft but it almost wrote itself. Later on I was able to send it to G.H.Q. for approbation, through Commander Crosbie, and Radio Eireann accepted it. Captain Seamus McCall, the chief Press Officer in Dublin, gave a lot of good advice and brought the army's assistance in providing sound effects. I had hoped for direct recordings from an M.T.B. but this was impossible so Captain McCall recorded army motor-cycles with fair results, but lacking in the shattering qualities of the original. The engine-room telegraphs were reproduced in the studio, the hooter was recorded from chord a played on a small organ – not very successfully – and rifle-fire was recorded from a rifle-range. The final explosion beat us until P.P. Maguire, the producer, and a very brilliant, painstaking and resourceful producer too, discovered an explosion recorded during an attack on an Atlantic convoy. The feature was called *Routine Job* and I was asked to write a version of it for *An Cosantoir*, one of the army papers. I think it gives some slight idea of what we were up to in those days I am reproducing it.

A drifting mine.

October Winds (as in 'The Castle of Dromore') lamented around Kilmain Head Look-Out Post at the dreary hour between four and five a.m. and it was 'The Castle of Dromore' that the Watcher off duty was trying to play on a mouth-organ, sitting inside by the fire and wondering if he would sound like Larry Adler if he got one of those chromatic affairs. Outside, the Watcher on duty – glasses to his eyes – was now quite certain that what he was looking at was a drifting mine. He rapped sharply on the window and Mac, his mate, stuck his head out with more than a little grumbling. After all, it *was* his hour to be in and it was a raw, damp morning, visibility not up to much, a bit of a sea and a cold wind.

'Well?' he said, patiently. The other man, keeping his glasses to his eyes, indicated the direction of the mine. Propping the telescope against a window-frame Mac focussed and searched. After days and days of a steady south-easterly blow it was certain there would be mines – plenty of them – and drifting right into the way of the coastal traffic. Yes, there it was. Another of them. Then things began to happen swiftly. The position of the mine was noted, together with wind and weather, and Mac turned the ringer – maliciously pleased to get Miss Clery, at the exchange, out of bed.

'Defence call,' he announced, adding 'Priority' with all the emphasis created by a cold winter morning.

The switchboard operator at Command H.Q. was the next link in the chain of events, juggling with plugs and cords, he invoked the Duty Officer and after that Mac, in his chilly concrete hut, went into a huddle with his superior – fifty miles away – while Mac's mate supplied additional details of drift and speed. That was all that concerned the L.O.P. at the moment but not all that concerned the unsuspecting mine. A further fifty miles from the Duty Officer the Marine Service Depot Duty Petty-Officer was sitting by the fire wondering how soon tea would be up in the Guard Room. At a switchboard set the Marine Service operator was working out something that looked like noughts and crosses but was really a calculation on a calendar to see if he would be on 'phone duty on Christmas Day. An indicator fell with a little click and a sharp buzz interrupted the great work.

'Duty Officer? Hold on, sir,' and presently the Duty Officer at Command was passing on his information to the Duty Officer at the Marine Service Depot. So the report went through, gathering a little detail and a little instruction and finally becoming an order which the Duty Petty Officer carried to the M.T.B. on duty. His way led him to the basin where the M.T.B.s lay, squat lumps of blackness except for a faint glow in the wheel-house of each. Even in the basin the wind made little waves slap crossly against their sides. Yes, a wretched morning; that cup of tea in the Guardroom would be very welcome.

M.T.B.s in Haulbowline basin.

'Halt! Who goes there?' (Though the sentry on deck would have known the sound of that P.O.'s boots anywhere.) The message changed hands and the Commanding Officer of the M.T.B. received it, roughly recalled from dreams of Buenos Aires to early morning in Haulbowline.

'Call the C.P.O.' But the C.P.O. was already up, roused in his quarters opposite the Wardroom and struggling into a thick sweater.

'We're going out, C.P.O. Kilmain Head. Another of them.' It was not necessary to ask another of what.

'What's the weather like?' said the skipper, swinging his legs out of his bunk. It was not necessary to ask that either. The sentry's oilskins, the slight motion of the ship, and the temperature, were the answer. The Engineer officer raised himself in the top bunk and groaned. What a life! Drenched on deck or gassed below. What a life! But the news was music to the sentry for his duties were finished and he could retire to his blankets and to the sleep which only good sentries sleep when resting off guard.

The C.P.O. roused his crew by the simplest possible means, he pressed down the alarm which sounded in the forecastle and before they had time to ask what was the matter he was down among them to say that they were getting up at once and would the cook please get some tea on. But this was different. The cook on duty had every respect for the C.P.O.'s rating but there some things even C.P.O.s could not interfere with, the cook was one of them and tea was another. Tea at five in the morning! And then he went into his act, improvising on his favourite theme of 'I'm acting as cook, I am, but I'm not a so-and-so conjurer.' He politely asked whether the C.P.O. had a private stock of tea. No? Then there could be no tea, Chief. Of course, if the crew wished, they could have their breakfast tea now and no tea at breakfast, but – tea at five in the morning *and* at breakfast, ah no; he was an acting cook, he was, not a *bewildered* conjuror. And during this tirade he was busy lighting the spirit-cups below the burners while the crew outside his galley dragged on sea-boots and jerseys.

In the Engine Room the Engineer officer and his P.O. gazed at each other across the four enormous engines with a kind of evil understanding, as if they were about to destroy the universe. The P.O. appeared to move a small lever rapidly, the officer moved something down by the compressed-air bottles, there was a high-pitched groaning sound, followed by a shattering explosion. The Port Forward engine was roaring out the news that an M.T.B. was going out on the job again and more than one sleeper in the other craft roused, and cursed. Then the other engines were quickly started off the first.

By now each member of the crew was at his particular work. The port-holes were closed. Rifles and ammunition were brought up on deck and placed in the Action Shelter. The outgoing signal lights were run up. The steering was tested and the moorings were singled off. In the pause while the engines were warmed up mugs of tea were hastily swallowed, tea which successive duty-cooks had managed to scrape and save for just such a rainy day.

The C.P.O. waited at the wheel, his head above the windshield, and beside him waited the skipper. They agreed gloomily that it looked dirty, *was* dirty in fact, and would very likely be worse before it was better. Then a hooter sounded and a small loud-speaker gave its version of the Engineer officer's voice announcing that they were O.K. in the Engine Room.

By means of a boat-hook the bows were swung out, away from the wall. 'Ting-ting,' the engine-room telegraph rang sharply as the M.T.B. nosed cautiously towards the entrance. 'Ting-ting,' the four asynchronous exhausts became one vast grumble. 'Ting-ting,' and as she cleared the entrance her bows rose up, her wake fanned out behind her and the water turned white as she headed for the open sea.

Back in Kilmain Head Look-Out Post it was now Mac's turn to be outside and he kept watching the mine for it was inclined to drift a little and the moon which had showed it up was now clouding over. His mate measured the distance to the Marine Service Base, calculated the probable delay in getting the report through, did a little mental arithmetic, decided that something ought to be showing up and went outside again. Something which might have been a breaker but was not, something smashing the short steep seas apart – its navigation lights hardly visible against the sky, something was coming from the west.

The M.T.B.'s decks streamed with water and so did the oil-skins and sea-boots of the two look-outs stationed in the bows. The motion was decidedly uncomfortable, something like a high-speed elevator driven by a demented attendant with no very fixed purpose in life. Compared with this a patrol-vessel's motion was positively majestic. But everything was well-secured above and below decks, and if she was pounding a bit – well, the deck-heads were padded with rubber.

The skipper rang for half-speed and the sinister engineers talked in sign language because speech was almost impossible.

'We're just on the bearing the L.O.P. gave us,' the skipper glanced up from the compass. As he spoke a Lucas light winked from the grey bulk of Kilmain Head.

'It-is-half-a-mile-south-west-of-you.'

'Or that's where it ought to be,' said Mac to his mate when the M.T.B.'s brilliant Aldis lamp acknowledged his message and the ship swung away to starboard and again reduced speed.

The mine, standing barely three feet out of the water, was hard to pick out in the confused sea, particularly from the low decks. One of the look-outs got it first.

'Mine on the Port bow, sir! About a cable's length.' A sea threw it up, a spiked and pot-bellied shape momentarily sharp against the brightening sky. The engine-room telegraph moved to Stand-By and then to Stop and the two engineers relaxed slightly and felt better now that the steep planing angle had subsided. A Leading-Seamen and two seamen took up their positions in the bows with their rifles.

Shooting at a mine from an M.T.B.

'Only fire when you're sure. Don't waste ammunition in this light,' ordered the Skipper and they settled down to watch for the moment when the mine would rise against their foresights.

Crack! ... Clunk! metal struck metal.

Crack! ... Clunk! Two hits in two, not bad but not altogether good because they were high hits, admitting less water to sink the mine than a hit on the waterline would have done. For a full minute there were no more hits, only derisive plops in the water. By then the M.T.B. was too close for safety so the Skipper ordered his men to hold their fire while he circled into a new position, giving the mine as much of his wash as he could so as to help in filling it.

Crack! ... and the eerie dying shriek of a ricochet over the noise of the sea.

There was light enough by this time for the Coast Watchers to get a good view of the work. The sea was now on the beam and the M.T.B. was rolling very violently; the men rested their rifles against a torpedo-tube. Three more good hits and it was necessary to circle again. This time the seas were right aft and the background of the still grey Western sky was not very good. The Skipper considered the position through his glasses. She was certainly going. Her motion was sluggish owing to the amount of water she had taken in, but she was going very slowly and the Poor Farmers' petrol was being used up steadily below. Furthermore the engineers had some reason against keeping the engines idling too long.

'What do you think, C.P.O?'

'She's going all right, sir. We're in a good position now, steadier then we've been yet.'

'Yes,' said the Old Man, 'let her have it again.'

The men reloaded and moved forward cautiously, two of them resting their rifles on the wire rail and the third steadying his at the anchor-davit. As A.B. John Byrne took first pressure something told him that this would be the last shot. He did not aim at any particular part of the mine, other than the waterline, but he knew that his next would be *the* shot. There she was ... up! Now down ... now rising again to complete a rendezvous with his .303 bullet. He squeezed the trigger and had his reward.

First a dull red flash, then a black cloud and simultaneously a tremendous roar, followed by a hot acrid wind and a violent shock throughout the whole craft. Then complete silence, seas breaking silently on deafened ears.

'Any souvenirs, lads?' gasped the cook, sticking his head up through the hatch.

'Get your head down out of that or you'll have a souvenir through it!' snapped the L/S. The three men resisted the temptation to look up at the sky and wished that they could draw themselves under their helmets like tortoises.

Then the souvenirs began to arrive; nasty jagged souvenirs, hissing into the sea and thumping on the deck here and there.

After what seemed a long time the shower ceased, the cloud of smoke and vapour drifted away, the sea ceased to boil and a number of dead cod came to the surface, astounded out of their lives by the greatest shock known to cod society.

'Unload!' said the Leading-Seamen. He hadn't hit a thing himself.

Well, that was that. The Coast Watchers made their report by telephone, the Officer Commanding the M.T.B. made his report by radio, the ship came round in a tremendous sweep and raced westwards before the rising sun.

Another mine had been removed. It would never more lie in the track of the shipping. It would never go foul of a fisherman's nets. It would never drift into a bay and cause the evacuation of an entire village – if the village had the good fortune to be awake. It would never destroy. It had been destroyed and life and property had been rendered safe by the carrying out of what became a routine job of co-operation between the Coast Watching Service and the Marine Service.

The Lieutenant stepped down into the Chart-Room, switched on the rotary Clear-Vues which kept the spray off the windows and lit his first cigarette of the day. The C.P.O. relieved him on the little bridge and below in the forecastle all hands – for some reason – were giving their attention to insulting the cook and aspersing his sex-life. He, however, was singing South of Border, his only song, and anyhow the roar of the Primus jets prevented him from hearing anything. The forecastle was pleasantly warm, oilskins were hung up to drain off. Everyone was in good humour. One more mine down, not so many rounds used on it either, and good shooting in a bad sea. More important still, breakfast was on its way. Ah, the sausages! Ah, the bacon! … and maybe a little bit of liver saved from yesterday. It was almost worth the cold and discomfort.

Then they all remembered that it was Friday.

10

In Dock

Let me tell you about my operation – not that it amounted to that but there seems to be a leaning in all of us towards discussing medical and surgical matters and my opening phrase, which Peter Arno made immortal, is as good a lead-in to the subject as any. Perhaps there is a bit too much I in all this, but as I am the line to which I have secured all these short-ends of Marine Service experience then I must occur more than a little. This chapter and the next deal with matters more army than Marine Service but they are experiences which came the way of many of us.

In January 1942 I was back in the *Muirchu* and we were ordered out on Port Control duty, providing a base for the examination crews. This duty was usually carried out by Port Control Personnel from their station on a jetty below Fort Camden but a heavy gale had made their quarters look rather silly so we had to look after them for a short period, alternating with the *Fort Rannoch*. Almost as soon as we anchored the weather began to deteriorate again and a southerly gale blew up and lasted for days, with the ship rolling uncomfortably and mostly lying across the channel. An anchor-watch was necessary at night, especially as a fair amount of signals were passed to us from the Forts, and as we were without a Warrant-Officer I had to carry out this job myself. The final arrangement was that I should go on watch every night from midnight until 8 a.m. and have the day off and a very nice arrangement too (I am extremely partial to lying in bed) if the weather had not been so bad at night. All night and all day it blew and rained. One particularly bad night I had the old man called, Lieutenant Hamilton, it was, and I remember having the most improbable and extraordinary conversation I ever had with anyone at sea as we walked up and down the bridge.

But in the end my wet uniforms never really dried, I caught cold, tried to fight it off for a day, and then 'went sick'. I wasn't inclined to eat and the Medicine Chest did not do me much good; Mist: Expect:, Mist: Stim:, Mist:

Sed:, Mist: Alba:, Mist: Diarrh; I don't know what Longmore brought me, everything except Tinct: Iod: on a feather. An officer came below and took my temperature. 'Ah,' he said, unconcernedly, looking up from the thermometer, 'these things are never really accurate.'

The next thing I recall is hearing the anchor being let go and being told that we had anchored off Cobh. A doctor and a medical orderly came on board and I was told that I was to go to hospital by ambulance. Immediately I was filled with a sort of idiotic self-importance and told Longmore that I could never make the companionway and would have to be brought on deck in a stretcher.

'I'll get the Boatswain to make a special one,' he said obligingly. Then I started to dress very slowly, putting my clothes on over my pyjamas and laughing as I did so; I recall all this because I thought I was laughing at someone else. Forgetting my insistence on a stretcher, I emerged on deck, a gaunt and unshaven figure, and was over the side and into the launch before Longmore was ready with the blankets he was warming to put round me. The crew of the launch looked rather concerned and this blew up my importance still more. I was led to an ambulance and put to bed on a stretcher with hot-water bottles. A stretcher at last, this was the real thing!

Then there was a long wait and the tyranny and selfishness of the sick developed further in me when I was told that we were waiting for another customer – as if I wasn't a matter of life or death. P.O. Tim Gillan climbed into the ambulance to see how I was. He pointed out that as we were waiting very near a hotel a hot whiskey would be a good thing before the journey. I didn't want it. And brandy would be better still, said Tim, hot or cold. Somehow there seemed to be something in this, I half sat up on the stretcher.

'Ah, no,' said the Army Medical Corps sergeant entering the ambulance and pushing me down. 'It wouldn't do.'

A stretcher now slid into the other side of the ambulance bearing something covered with blankets and an oilskin. I sat up again and uncovered its face to see if it was alive, it was a seaman – breathing but unknown to me.

The journey seemed very slow and I stirred restlessly.

'We're nearly there,' said the sergeant soothingly. Nearly there! As if I couldn't see the tops of the trees at Belvelly Bridge passing the window and showing that we were not even halfway.

We swung into Collins Barracks, Cork, and stopped at the hospital. The seaman was carried away on his stretcher and I was invited to walk. Walk! Not a bit of it. The stretcher idea was firmly in my mind and I insisted on being carried to the ward. Here I was gently transferred to a bed and orderlies started to undress me. I again laughed as I appreciated my amazing cleverness in keeping my pyjamas on under everything. Next, more hot-water bottles. Next, a doctor. Next an A.M.S. corporal beside me, with forms. Yes – once more it was name, rank, age, religion. Daily rate of pay? Three pounds a day, I told him. He sighed resignedly and abandoned the cross-examination. Then a fizzy drink, the prick of an injection, sleep and nightmares. These lasted only two nights really, but it seemed ages. I am told that the first time I opened my mouth was to suggest to the Ward in general that one man should stay awake on watch, in turn, to scare away the things at night. When half-awake I used to see, by some trick of the light, a terrible old man appearing against the opposite wall. Then I thought I saw Lennox Robinson and complained to him about this monster.

'But you're quite wrong,' said Lennox, 'he's a most delightful old person and he lives in Sandymount.' That finished the old man. And then, suddenly, I was awake and feeling well and quite, quite furious with the Hospital, and with myself for getting there, and because I was not the whole centre of attention. I used to look at the seaman next to me and see just one baleful eye over the sheets.

'How long do you intend staying here?' asked the doctor.

'That depends on how I like it, sir,' I was surprised to hear myself saying. 'Does it? Well, don't you worry. We'll see to it that you don't like it too much,' he answered sharply. One freezing night when the heating broke down completely that M/O turned-to with a fatigue party clearing and re-stoking the furnaces and he did not leave the wards until they were at the correct temperature.

The surrounding Barracks seemed to cast its influence over the Hospital and the routine was carried out to a precise military time-table. Mallow Military Hospital, where I sojourned some years later, is a bright and encouraging hospital out in the country, and there the routine is less formal but quite smooth-running. Life, in Cork, began at 6.45 with, of all things, a roll-call. This was followed by the taking of temperatures and then, for the bed-patients, some breakfast and washing – in that order. After that there was a tremendous sweeping and polishing before the trolly of jingling Mists! Tincts! and Ungs! was pushed round.

The up-patients then turned-to with the lead-swinger – a lead weight hinged on the end of a pole and covered with felt which rubbed in the polish on the floor. At 10.30, 'Stand to your beds!' and the doctor made his visit to the Ward. After that came syphons of lemonade and bottles of stout for those ordered to take it, soup at half-past eleven and lunch at one. I decided, when in bed, to refuse all food – to spite the hospital, I thought maliciously. The seaman beside me – whose name was Kelly – would not eat either.

'Why won't you take your lunch?' asked an Army Medical Corps sergeant, sent by the sister.

'I don't want to.'

'I know why. Our food here isn't as good as yours.' I felt embarrassed.

'No, sarge, it's not that, I just don't want it.'

'I know your rations at sea are better than ours, I'm sorry we can't do more for you.' I felt more uncomfortable still.

'I'm sure the food's grand, it's not that, I just don't feel like eating.'

'Ah, no. The trouble is that it isn't good enough for you,' he said sadly. 'I'll tell you what, Chief. Just try little of this, just a matter of form to please the Sister, just pretend to eat it. That sailor beside you is pretty weak and if he saw you eating he might try a bit himself – then you needn't eat anything more.' The sergeant handed me a rice pudding with jam on it. I finished it and he walked away grinning, thinking how easy it was to handle people if you went the right way about it. After that I took all my meals.

Lunch was followed by another general clean up, more medicine – including quantities of Cod Liver Oil – and more Lead-swinger. Tea came at four-thirty, and more cleaning up. Milk and biscuits came in the evening, another roll-call, and then we were settled for the night. The night-sister made her first rounds, said good-night after asking how each of us did and the radio was switched off. The radio seemed to be on continuously and 'Rose O'Day' was the maddening tune of the moment. A central set in Ward 1 controlled the loud-speakers in the Wards and as soon as one became interested in one programme one could be certain that another would be tuned in at the whim of Ward 1. The only items we got in their entirety were the News, the Hospitals Request Programme, Music While You Work and Question Time. For Question Time we each picked a number and only answered the questions given to that number. One team was in one row of beds and the other team in the opposite row. This is the best way of listening to Question Time. It is easy for the listener to feel, in a superior way, that he has answered every question. Let him confine himself to one number and then see if all the easy ones come his way.

It was pleasant lying in bed and looking at the light from the large windows shining on the restful green walls. There were a few good reproductions of religious pictures, opposite me was the central portion of Raphael's Madonna and Child.

After a week I asked for permission to get up and was allowed to do so. I dressed sitting on my bed, got my shaving things, took one step towards the bathroom and fell flat across the next bed. I had to learn that these things could not be done all at once, but by taking quarter days up and then half-days I was soon spending whole days up – and not enjoying them. When the bed-patient is tired of reading or has nothing to read he can put down his head and sleep. The up-Patient cannot do anything more than the bed-patient except visit other Wards if he is allowed to, or go into the city twice a week if he is well enough. In Mallow Hospital he can walk about the grounds and look at the Workhouse graveyard. The amount of nothing-to-do for a sailor or soldier in hospital, after he has carried out the mild fatigues imposed on him, is immense. He can't play chess or draughts or snakes and ladders indefinitely.

Some years later a medical officer asked me for a suggestion as to how some fund he had in hands might be well expended for the patients. It made me think considerably. The sum was not large enough to equip a recreation-room and in the end I suggested deck-chairs for the up-patients in the summer months, and really good libraries. The trouble, said the M/O, was the malingerer who 'went sick' at least twice a month and who aimed at staying in a comfortable hospital when he succeeded in getting there. Army doctors are skilled in spotting these men with moving pains in the small of the back but it is sometimes impossible for them to be absolutely sure of a case of malingering and because of these men, and because of genuine cases who might – perhaps unconsciously – retard their recovery by contrasting their too delightful surroundings with a barracks, it would not do to make hospital too much of a holiday.

The kindness of patient towards patient impressed me deeply. Possibly it was the result of having little else to do but each up-patient seemed to adopt a bed-patient and did everything for him, from shaving him, if necessary, to mysterious evolutions with 'pigeons' and the screens. It was something remote from service life, even from home life, something I had never seen before. Disparity in rank did not count, only a man's need.

Of the Nursing Sisters some were genial, picking up their patients' nick-names, others were more aloof, and all were considerate and seemed marvelously calm and pleasant in any emergency, whether at three in the afternoon or three in the morning.

There was the usual variety of characters in Each Ward. Though hospital blues tended to standardise the appearance, men did not put off their old selves through being ill; rather, illness seemed to intensify personal characteristics and the Cribber, the Tough Guy, the Funny-man and the Student were quickly diagnosed. The most amazing type was the Medical Expert. This man was usually an up-patient, convalescing from something obscure and perpetually on the verge of being marked-out of hospital. He was well-in with the sister, somehow had access to the Medical History Sheets (Army Form 30) and knew everything about everyone. One of these experts assured me that in a hospital he would not name there was a ward full of what he called 'Military lunatics' and the M/O could only enter it with an armed guard.

'You're a hundred-and-two to-night,' the Medical Expert would say, 'but don't let that worry you at all, I was a hundred-and-three myself for a fortnight, heard the M/O telling the Sister he'd put me in a bunk by myself next day – hadn't a hope for me.'

At other times he would hoarsely mutter, 'Do you see that young corporal there? If they can get his temperature down two nights running they're going to open him, and mark my words they'll find more inside him than they're looking for. *I know what I'm talking about.* I had the same myself, they brought the greatest specialists to me and still they didn't know what ailed me, but *I* knew – and I still know – put your hand there, do you feel that? I'll tell you what they did for me – *word* all! Doctors! Vets, more likely. What were they in civvy life I'd like to know.'

One of these horrors hated fresh air and as I was senior N.C.O. in the Ward one of my duties was to see that the windows, which were operated by handles, were opened, to the width indicated by the Sister, and kept open. One night the Medical Expert appeared at my bedside in his hospital night-shirt, shivering in an exaggerated manner.

'We'll all be frozen in our beds, Chief.' I had been through this before.

'That man,' he pointed a shaking finger to a patient who had an oxygen apparatus beside him, 'that man is in the crisis of pewmonia [sic]. You'll have his blood on your head.'

'Get back to bed.' He padded away.

'Oh, God!' he groaned, making his bed rattle with his shivering, 'I won't see this night through. Chief, you'll have my death on your conscience too. I'm going to get permission from the night-sister to dress and sleep in my clothes. Oh, good God … Oh, good God!'

I was talking one evening to a seaman who had come in with a collar-bone broken while playing Rugby. He was trying to date some recent Depot happening and he said, 'It was the same day as you were promoted.'

'Promoted?'

'The day you were promoted to Warrant-Officer.'

'Did you see this in orders?' No, he hadn't exactly *seen* it, nor had another seaman in the Ward, but they both knew about it, everyone knew about it. Another ball-hop? Yet it had happened in the unexpected way that everything did happen. I would look rather foolish if I telephoned the Depot and it turned out not to be true so I telephoned what was then the great centre of all Service information, the Imperial Hotel in Cobh, and announced myself.

'Congratulations!' said Peggy at once. That night I got leave to go over to the Sergeant's Mess in the barracks and carry out the ceremony of mildly 'wetting the stripe' – or, in my case, the gold ring. And so I exchanged the friendly title of 'Chief' for the harsher one of 'Warrant' – or 'D'bloo-oa' with the rising Cork inflection.

I was very well-treated in that Hospital, we were all well treated, and I made many friends there; the finest of them were those magnificent men who would never leave hospital and who knew the way they were going. They were the brightest and bravest and the most heart-breaking; their calm and resignation in the company of men who were in for just a few weeks with some trifling complaint was something I shall never forget.

I got some sick-leave and then rejoined the *Muirchu* in my new quarters and wearing my glitteringly new rings and cap-badge.

For a long time afterwards my thoughts used to turn to those men in Hospital who were leaving life. Only after the Rosary had been said and, for the others, sleep settled on the Ward, would they declare their inner minds by a restless stirring or by a long sigh in the darkness.

11

Shore Duty: Potential Officers' Course

Whenever things get into such a smooth groove that the passing of time is not noticed there comes a sudden jar and a jolt and everything has to be organised over again.

I came back off annual leave in the autumn of 1943 and settled down to my usual routine on board, the work being very slightly intensified in order to catch up on things that had occurred in my absence, and then, *poum!* – as the French comic papers say – the blow fell; 'You're going to Collins Barracks, Cork, on a potential Officers' Course.' Only a buzz, I couldn't get anything more than that until the very day before my departure, and then the Aldis lamps began to blink and the semaphore flags to wave and the radio to whistle and I was hustled over to the Depot – hustled here and hustled there and hustled back to the ship again. 'You're for Collins Barracks to-morrow, with C.P.O. O'Mahony.' The date, time and place was all I got out of the Depot – and the best rifle I could draw from the Armourer.

C.P.O. O'Mahony was the first Stroke the Marine Service Rowing Club ever had. We met in the train on the way up to Cork and started to discuss the future. What amazed us was that we were being sent on a purely military course at a time when an interesting navigation course was about to start in the School of Navigation. Perhaps we were not amazed – by that time no one was really amazed at anything that happened – but we raised our eyebrows a little and felt green uniforms creeping round us. Later we learned that we had been accepted for promotion by the Marine Service as far as their end of the matter went but the important military training requirements had to be satisfied.

We took a taxi up the winding hill to where Collins Barracks squats above the city of Cork and catches every wind that blows and when the metal door slammed behind us there began the most wretched period of my life in the Service; the only period, when one excludes Coast Watching. I suppose I entered the Barracks with memories of my pleasant course in Collins Barracks, Dublin, but I was soon to find that all this was different. After the inevitable questionnaire of name, rank, age etc. we went to the room in the Block assigned to the Course. It was a long rectangle with windows on either side and it had just been re-decorated, that is to say the wall was made of wet cement for nearly half-way up – one could push a finger into it – and the water dribbled out of this and down to the floor, soaking into our uniforms during the following months. For light we had a stable-lantern, the electrician was too busy. There were bed-boards.

This is not a typical barrack-room, but it was our room and, we shared it with ten others. One of the first things Ned O'Mahony and I were told to do was to ascertain the cubic capacity of the room and divide it by the number of beds to see that there was sufficient air per man.

'Watch this closely,' said the little sergeant in charge to a group of soldiers who had arrived for the Course. 'You might be called on to do it yourselves at any moment.'

We measured, multiplied and divided and the soldiers eyed us with dislike. The result of our calculations did not agree with the sergeant's figure of what it should be,

'But that's all been reduced since the Emergency,' he said. Then we explored. We saw the lavatories, from which the doors had been removed. We saw the dank wash-house which we were to share with the Construction Corps and where there was cold water only. Why should it be assumed that these conditions are good enough for a soldier, that he doesn't really need hot water in the mornings, not even when icicles hang from the leaky taps?

We learned that the Potential Officers' Course would last for, at the very least, three months and that the successful soldiers would then proceed to the Military College at the Curragh to do it all again, with embellishments. We also learned that we would be moving around from Reveille at 7 a.m. until the conclusion of Supervised Study at 7 p.m., with additional time to be added for our private work. Three months of that course easily beat nine months Coast Watching for unpleasantness. Maybe these astringents are good for us and make us appreciate how pleasant our normal lives really are.

Naturally the Course did not start for a week after our arrival, after all the hurry. During this time men arrived from other military posts and Ned and I worked up some of the military subjects about which we knew *word* all.

One day I looked across the Square at an Officer walking by.

'I don't think I'd like to have that man as O/C of the Course,' I said idly.

'Well, as it happens, that man is going to be our O/C,' said a sergeant beside me, and the Potential Officers' Course began with a roar. Yes, he was our O/C, a dark and tall Captain, and we all referred to him as Joe. I began the Course with an active objection to that officer which turned to the greatest respect. He appeared to regard us all as criminals and, as such, treated us strictly in accordance with justice. There was no favouritism. There were no concessions, we simply got what he deemed to be our due. Sometimes he allowed himself a bitter smile at some appalling ineptitude, at other times he would probe into us after latent knowledge in a most painstaking way. His first question to me in a class was to detail the organization of a Motor Squadron; it had been part of our home-work.

'A Motor Squadron is organised into Squadron Headquarters, one armoured troop and three motor troops, sir.'

'Yes. Go on, W/O. Give me the Headquarters Organisation.'

'I don't know any more, sir.' There I was, standing up among about fifty soldiers and one other sailor in a clammy hut with icicles hanging through the roof, my thighs against a table, a bench against the backs of my knees. What in hell, did I need to know about a Motor Squadron?

'I don't know any more, sir.'

'You don't know any more?' slowly from Joe. 'Who commands the Squadron H.Q.?'

'I don't know, sir.'

'You don't know.' He lit a cigarette. 'You may all smoke.'

So this was going to be a long inquisition.

'Who do you think commands it, W/O?'

'I don't know, sir.'

'Guess! Guess, man, guess!'

'A commandant, I suppose, sir.'

'You suppose. Of course, it's a commandant. No supposing about it. Who is 2 I/C?' If the O/C is a commandant the 2 I/C is probably a captain.

'A captain.'

'Correct – go on, who comes, next?' After a captain a lieutenant, I supposed. How many of them? Can't remember so I slur the number and make it sound like, 'Mmmm lieutenants, sir.'

'How many?'

'... er ... two.'

'And what are these two lieutenants?'

'Adjutant, sir,' this was safe anyway. Motor Squadron; oh, yes ...

'... and Technical.'

'Yes, and who else?'

'I don't remember, sir.'

'Who keeps them fed and clothed?'

'Oh, Quartermaster.' And so on we went through the Company Sergeant and the C.Q.M.S., the Sergeant-Fitter, the Sergeant-Fitter (Signals), and Corporal (Clerk) and the Corporal (Cook) down through the Baker, the Tailor, the Shoemaker, the Storemen, the Technical Storemen etc, etc, the eight drivers M/T, the two Trumpeters and the four General Duties. By vaguely remember-ing past work, by prompting and by tooth-pulling from Joe I stumbled along through this essential part of a potential naval officer's knowledge.

'So you did know it, after all,' said Joe, at last. 'Why did you say you didn't?' What a completely ridiculous position. I muttered something at him.

'Sit down. Next man, yourself – corporal. Give me the attachments to a Motor Squadron H.Q.'

Once in a spell, once in a wildly infrequent interlude in the long spells of dreariness, Joe would finish his class slightly early, throw down his notes, and say 'Any cribs?' Neither Ned nor I ever cribbed because we had made the stupendous discovery that the Course was to the soldiers on it, and particularly to the privates, merely an extension of their usual military routine, a university after a school, a transfer from an outpost to a city. The day's routine was almost normal to them; so, with improvements, were the four rooms we occupied in the Block, so were the wash-house and the lavatories. In fact, the soldiers were actually enjoying the course. Ned and I decided that we must bow our heads to the storm. The absence of electric light was occasionally mentioned, working by the light of a storm lantern was a bit of a strain and we had to work by this light for a long time, but everything else seemed just part of the system so we said nothing. The soldiers, on the other hand, cribbed about everything imaginable – and they knew how to do it; they knew their rights even if it was only the traditional right to twenty-seven inches in the ranks, the only right a soldier is supposed to have, everything else being acts of clemency on the part of his commanding officer. Much of the cribbing was ingenious 'talking for the sake of talking' and Joe was very quick at cutting through this and making his man look rather foolish.

In that horrid class-room we studied Military Organisation, Administration, the Duties of The Orderly Officer and many other subjects, including Military Law, which taught me the consequences of attempting to sell my ship or of Wilfully Impressing Carriages and Their Attendants. We also had Courts Martial, Anti-Gas, Chemical Warfare, Map Reading (at which Ned and I scored heavily) and Hygiene and Sanitation. Twice running in our Hygiene and Sanitation lectures we were given instruction in the treatment of that well known menace to life aboard ship, Snake-bite. We also learned how to dig latrines, going out to the Camp Field for the purpose and then refilling the holes and, out of broken chamber pots, making head stones inscribed with the names of our instructing officers and N.C.O.s.

This dreadful plateau, the Camp Field, lay across the road from the Barracks. During our early-morning visits to it Cork was submerged, a valley of mist with the city spires probing through it. It was nearly always intensely cold and extremely muddy there. Here we did the Battle Course. Another Camp Field diversion was the Barrack Square form of Platoon Battle-Drill. In this we moved from point to point in a sort of skeletonised theoretical attack. In order to drive the movements home each fresh one was announced by such slogans as, 'As for Battle-Drill, tell off!' 'Number one riflemen, number one bomber; number two riflemen, number two bomber.' And before we engaged our theo-retical enemy we bawled the sternly admonishing 'Cover! Crawl! Observe! *Fire!*' Our enemy was invariably a flag stuck in a bucket in a distant part of the field and, doggedly continuing to announce our intentions before each move-ment, we would shout 'Enemy at bucket. We will kill all enemy in that bucket.' It was unbelievably funny and at the same time entirely practical. First, the capture of an enemy post was illustrated on a blackboard. Then we followed the movements ourselves in the Camp Field. Finally, by constantly going through skeletonised movements and yelling out our intentions the actual sequence of events in fighting in open country was driven into us for all time. Ned and I didn't like it but we did admire it as a method of instruction for soldiers and I was delighted to hear all the old slogans coming over the loudspeakers at the Military Tattoo at Ballsbridge. You remember the capture of the house? If you have read an excellent book called *A Walk in The Sun* you will have read a very good description of battle-drill applied to actual warfare.

Another resort of ours, of an afternoon, was Goulding's glen. Here we did a tougher version of the Battle-Course from which possible foot-trouble excused me from the intermediate running, though I did all the individual obstacles. After going over the course we usually fell out for a long smoke, with our instructors posted round us watching for officers. That was in the days when the first ferocity of the course had worn off. White's Cross and points around it was another rendezvous of ours. White's Cross sacred to Map Reading, Camouflage, Fire Orders and an exercise called Individual Stalk in which selected men gave their version of how they would approach a certain spot, making the utmost use of cover. They were then sent on their stalk while the rest of us repaired to the spot indicated and swore to the stalkers that we had seen them all the time, that stampeding cattle had given them away, and any other thing we could think of to annoy men who had been crawling through bog-drains and ditches to justify their own theories of how the spot might be surprised. The Glen and White's Cross were never entirely disagreeable, nor were our cross-country rides with the maps but, according to the wind at the time, the Camp Field took turns with a locality known as the 'Back of the Band Hut' at being the most abominable spot – and the Barrack Square was a close second. I am sure we did twelve hours every week at the Back of the Band Hut. This place of torment was a gravel walk behind a brick parapet and it commanded the whole of the immediate hinterland of Cork City and received every wind that blew, from West to North East. Here we did Recognition of Difficult Targets (With Aids) and by this means we directed the fire of a section on a Gable-end of House, Road Junction, Poplar, or, Lone Bushy-Topped Tree – not forgetting End of Hedgerow. The army recognises no wind force between 12 m.p.h. and 15 m.p.h. (Ned and I had the whole Beaufort Scale), its colour-range is limited too and it has only two trees, the Poplar and the Lone Bushy-Topped. Lone Bushy-Topped tree, it sounded so sad, I felt rather like one myself. Many a time I brought fire to bear on a Lone Bushy-Topped tree from the Back of The Band Hut. The key-word to the sequence of commands which produced this effect was DRINK: Designation, Range, Indication, Number of Rounds, Kind of Fire. The snag about key-words is that one can remember them but one can't always remember what each letter stands for. PRIDE spelt backwards gives the sequence of instruction; Explanation, Demonstration, Imitation, Repetition, Practice. But what does SARDINE stand for? Or FACTOR, spelt with an E, instead of an O?

Map-reading and Grenades were the only subjects I enjoyed on the course. Grenades we found to be simple and interesting and Ned O'Mahony and I were the best shots with a Grenade Discharger, but we couldn't throw one anywhere near the ring when using the official method of throwing; I believe one is allowed to throw in any manner now. Recently the ship was coming alongside and I heard a seaman with a heaving-line, mocking at some past military course, say to himself, 'Prepare to throw … throw!' and the coils made an arc between ship and shore.

Life on the Course began with Reveille, sometimes beautifully phrased and sometimes hesitantly, note by note. It always caused a slight stir followed by a profound silence as each man tried to snatch a few more moments of rest. I woke up once and sat up in bed trying to make out the time. I could not see the hands my watch but there were lights in the Officers' Mess across the Square. Good, I thought, they're still up. It's probably about one o'clock. I covered myself up warmly again and Reveille blew; the lights had been turned on by the Mess staff cleaning up.

Check-parade was our first appearance outside. For most of our time Check-Parade was carried out in darkness and I gave up attending it as soon as it became impossible to pick out anyone on the Square and I usually had my blankets folded and bed-boards stacked by the time the others came back. Eventually we had army beds. Then came washing and shaving in cold water, with the tap running because there were no plugs in many of the basins. There were usually two or three others waiting behind one for a basin, and how I envied the boys of the Construction Corps on those cold mornings; few of them had to shave at all. After the first sting of the water I found a cold-water shave as good as any, but washing off the mud of the Camp Field in the evenings was another matter. If I was crossing the square towards the Mess for breakfast at five minutes to eight I was in good time, for me. Breakfast was a good meal, in fact all our meals were good, and after breakfast there was a quick pull-through of the rifle, a polishing of shoes and a tidying up of one's own area of the room. Once in twelve days I was room-orderly. This meant sweeping out the room and clearing away the wood and turf ash of the night before, but the room-orderly was excused all parades.

We first paraded outside the billets for inspection by one of our two officers, Captain Spicer or Lieutenant Bransfield, and then we marched on to the Square for the first main parade of the day. This was usually ended by marching round and round in respirators to the sound of Under The Double Eagle, played by the Construction Corps band. I often felt that to be strictly fair the band should have blown their instruments through some special form of respirator. After that we were dismissed and fallen out for a smoke and to change into the rig appropriate to whatever we were going to do. It was also a chance to run through the prepared lesson which had been announced to us at Supervised Study the night before. We worked on a system of mutual instruction, which meant that everyone would be called on to give instruction in some parts of the subjects for the day. We might start with Ceremonial Guard Mounting. This brought me back to the early days in the Depot when, at one time, we studied this absorbing subject under an instructor who never managed to complete the changing of the guard because he always insisted on the old guard's handing over a prisoner and, as our numbers were small, he had to be an imaginary one. So there we used to stand listening to an involved description of the imaginary prisoner standing at an imaginary table on which were his personal imaginary effects, these always consisted of money, pay-book, Rosary beads, and boot-laces and braces because he had been drunk the night before. By that time our period was up and there we had to leave the unfortunate imaginary man with a bad hangover, standing in his unlaced boots and holding up his trousers. But in Collins Barracks we did a more realistic version of Guard Mounting and after that we would probably double to the Camp Field for Battle Drill and double back to the Hut for a lecture on the Demolition of Dangerous Blinds. A little Bayonet Fighting often rounded off the morning's work.

The afternoons were usually confined to one subject out in the country somewhere, Goulding's Glen or White's Cross. This brought us back in time for tea, with monstrous appetites, unless another lecture could be squeezed in, and after tea we made down our beds and then fell in for Supervised Study or a military Question Time from six to seven. We were then technically free but there was always a lot to write up in our note-books, lessons to be prepared for next day, or, perhaps, an hour spent in stripping and assembling a machine-gun with the help of an experienced hand. Even the most knowledgeable of the soldiers very seldom went out of Barracks and Ned and I did not go out from Monday to Saturday. At nine o'clock in the evening someone would go outside the gates to a shop with orders for cakes known as 'Wedges' or 'Submarines' and someone else would fill our mugs in the Canteen. Most of us were in bed and asleep by half-past ten and certainly the active life and early-to-bed early-to-rise routine made one feel amazingly well. Wednesdays and Fridays broke this routine. After lunch on Wednesdays we were paid and then, with our soap and towels, we paraded to the Bath House for hot showers. I fell in with most other things on the course but refused to join in the ceremony previous to the hot showers which meant lining up and presenting one's vest to A Medical Orderly who hopefully scanned it for lice-infestation while another ran his eye over one's cringing figure.

Once or twice we were taken from the hot showers to complete the afternoon with an hour's Recognition of Difficult Targets (With Aids) from the Back of The Band Hut.

On Fridays we stopped work of a military nature at about a quarter to four and turned-to at Interior Economy. This meant scrubbing out the rooms and washing and scraping the tables, benches and bed-boards with sand and water. Even the Construction Corps in the next Block had an easier time of it than we had when it came to Interior Economy. After tea and Supervised Study on Friday evenings we would set to work at our kits in preparation for next day's inspection. I only learned two useful things on the Course, military Law was one and how to carry out a Kit Inspection was another. At the beginning I found Saturday morning's kit inspection to be extremely alarming. We had kit inspections on board in the Marine Service but ships are not designed for laying out kits in the army fashion, so we used to concentrate on checking the state of a man's kit and the number of articles in it, and I was not obliged to lay down kit at all. But here rank did not count. On my course in Dublin I brought all my kit and found I did not need it; here I had not brought such purely sea-going articles as sea-boots and oilskins. Joe made a long and impressive pause by my bed and then he dealt with me, article by article, and very slowly. It took a long, long time and was a god-send to the others because he passed them quickly. Ned O'Mahony, who had spent a long time in the Depot, went sailing through. Captain Spicer's attitude towards me was pained and sorrowful. Next week there was no sorrow at all, just plain anger – scorp – liver.

And then I set to work. I completed my kit. I marked everything. I even, in derision, stitched tags like numeral pennants on my white lanyards. A friendly sergeant helped me and we devised a special lay-out for my kit and very well it looked. Joe stopped thoughtfully by my bed while I handed over the kit and then, without a word, he moved on to my neighbour; a soldier who had escaped so far and whose kit seemed to consist of little more than two field-dressings, a pair of socks and someone else's cap. The probing began.

'Are those your socks?' he lifted the shameful things on the end of a cane.

'Yes, sir.'

'Why isn't your number on them?' My neighbour gave a puzzled stare at the socks, as if he never before noticed the incredible omission.

'Don't know, sir.'

'Why don't you know?' The wretched corporal tried to think of something.

'Why? I'm waiting, corporal.'

'Too busy, sir.'

'At what?' Another silence.

'Didn't you tell me you had no deficiencies?'

'Yes sir.'

'Where are your shirts?'

'One on me, and one in the wash, sir.'

'And the third?'

'I had it a moment ago, sir … I …'

'Do you expect me to believe that?' An unanswerable question.

'Now, listen to me, corporal – pay attention, all of you.'

We stiffened beside our beds. 'If I ever see …' and then a general address began; we were Potential Officers – *Officers!*: … our kits were disgraceful, our rooms were abominably kept, our appearance was unspeakable and our work was extremely poor. Unless there was an all-round improvement at once … and then followed threats of cancelled passes, extra work, and no leave at Christmas.

When Christmas came Joe, unbelievably, told us that we had all worked very well and in all our time there I don't think he took disciplinary action against any of us. A few Saturday mornings with Captain Spicer and one began to get the general outline of what he wanted to be done. Our room was damp and ill-lit, but it shone with scrubbing. Our kits were Perfection and Friday nights were nights when no one ever went out. Then the steel stampers bit into leather to renew markings, the stencils were re-applied, the marking-tapes touched up; even an un-numbered comb could cause trouble. Scraping my boot-brushes white with a razor blade annoyed me so much after a few weeks that I set about collecting a double kit, one for using and one for showing on inspections.

Any man in doubt about his appearance on the Commanding Officer's inspection on Saturday mornings always tried to get beside Ned or myself because the attention of the Major and the Commandant was always drawn away to our Number One uniforms and the condition of the beautiful rifles we had brought from the Depot.

Saturday was a half-holiday for Ned and me, though some of the others were always kept on Saturday and Sunday for exercises with the L.D.F. Oh, the rapture of Saturday! The giving out of the week-end passes and the indecent rush we used to make for the Barrack gates. On Saturdays we almost thought well of the Course and talked about the amusing incidents of the week and the interesting work and how nice everyone was. The *Muirchu* was nearly always alongside at Cobh at the week-ends so I was able to sleep on board. An evening in the Mess on Saturday and then a long rest on Sunday.

But returning by the first train on Monday Morning was the dismal conclusion of it all; the reaction was proportionate to our joy at leaving the Barracks on Saturday. Going away was good like most beginnings, but as soon as one reached Cobh one knew that Monday was rushing along. And then suddenly Monday was there and one was stumbling along the quay through the darkness to catch the train, to do one's homework by melancholy gas-light in a cold compartment still smelling of Saturday night's drunks. The zig-zag climb up to the Barracks with night still clinging to the heights, and the futile conversations.

'Well, at the worst there can't be more than nine weeks of it to go now, eight next Saturday.' Not much consolation in that with the buglers above us splitting the winter dawn and the boots of the returning soldiers striking sparks as they clashed up the steep hill.

I had three slight breaks during the Course. One was a few days' leave at Christmas, another was the unexpected arrival in Barracks of a unit of the March of Time. I had worked for the March of Time before and now here I was talking to Len Lye and wearing a Marine Service cap and blue dungarees, with a bayonet hopping up and down against my behind. My third was a trip to Dublin for recordings and rehearsals of a radio-documentary of mine called *Seaman*. It was not a good script, too over-laden with matter and consequently hard to handle. My experience now is that a radio script needs infinitely more handling than film script. Having dispensed with visuals the mind tends to elaborate a theme in all manner of ways. I take great pleasure in listening to radio plays and providing all the settings and costumes out of my own head – as every listener does – but with it all is the risk that the author may make too great demands on the listener. Television will limit production possibilities in one direction and open them up in another and I suppose we will lament it as we lamented the coming of sound films.

P.P. Maguire made the very best he could out of the two performances of *Seaman* but only one incident still remains with me. One night I had heard the lads in the Depot billets singing, quite spontaneously, before Lights Out. Very sweetly and sadly they were singing Carry Me Back to Old Virginny. I introduced this into my script and I think this sequence was effective. I listened to it in the Waiting Room of the Broadcasting Station and, when he heard the singing, one of the policemen who are always on duty there touched me on the arm and said, 'If you'd had them singing some old come-all-ye I'd never have forgiven you.' Neither of us meant that an old come-all-you would never be heard in the billets, but Carry Me Back was what I heard them singing that night and it seemed exactly right to me and to the policemen too, apparently.

After Christmas our examinations began and the Interview Board arrived. first we had the interview before The Interview. This interview, was a short one with Colonel Hanrahan, O/C Southern Command. And even before that we had a ferocious inspection. As the colonel's interview was held late in the day many of us were beginning to show a suspicion of bristle.

'There is still half an hour before you see the Colonel,' said our C/S Gene Meaney, thumbs in belt and teetering on his heels, 'Some of you go and shave all of your faces, all of you go and shave some of your faces.'

The Interview proper took two days. There was a long table at which the Board sat and a solitary chair was placed in front of it, just so far away that one had to strain one's ears very slightly to catch every word the quiet voices spoke.

Name, rank ... once more the particulars were given. Then, answering a steady succession of questions, one traced one's history up to the time of entering the Board Room. Why was I on a military course? I don't Know sir. And neither did they. Question on rifle-marksmanship, only partly answered. I am given the correct answer by Colonel Collins-Powell, and the number in the Training Regulations of the relevant page.

Another voice: 'Do you consider that every man in your crew should be familiar with the use of machine guns?'

'All deck-personnel anyhow, sir.'

'Why?'

'Because our machine guns are unprotected and when the first crew are knocked out others must be prepared to take over.'

Twice a Personage had said (once in my hearing), referring to our lack of gun-shields '... but in the heat of battle you won't notice their absence.' That had been a hell of a consolation to us.

The officers are looking at each other. The President says, 'All right, that'll do.' Cap on. Salute. Door opens, closes. Captain Spicer.

'What did they ask you?'

To my utter amazement I passed that Course. I think fourteen of us passed out of fifty-seven and most of them are army officers now. No Marine Service promotions were made, in fact there have never been any promotions from non-commissioned to commissioned rank on deck in the Service except for two officers who held Board of Trade Certificates. These were Ensign Flannery, who explained me my duties in the *Muirchu* when we met in Spike Island, and S/Lieut Barrett, who was always willing to throw everything aside (even his piano-accordion) to help in my work for an examination in Navigation and Seamanship which has been held over my head for nearly five years and which has never come off.

[It was on S/lieut Barret's promotion in 1942 that I stepped into the rank of Warrant-Officer which he vacated. (I don't know why this sentence was deleted. Ed.)]

So that was the Course, and I emerged from it improved in mind and body, if not in estate. I liked my companions on it very much and I liked some of the subjects; when a subject interested me, such as the Light Automatic, Military Law, or Map Reading I could give my heart to it but when faced with the organisation of a Howitzer Battery my brain closed up – a rather elaborate way of saying that I liked what I liked and what I did not like I disliked.

12

Resumed Patrol

It has recently become the custom in our Mess on board to eat a stuffed bullock's heart when our various courses lead us anywhere eastwards of Cobh. I don't know how the custom began but I feel that there must be something compensating and consoling in that bullock's heart which makes up to us for an easterly patrol. There is nothing good in an easterly patrol. If the weather is bad the land is invisible and from the Tuskar northwards one rolls along through short discoloured seas between the snarling banks; everything runs with water. In fine summer weather the land is also invisible under a woolly heat-haze, mad refractions occur off Braun Head, and the Patent Log, the echometer and the Direction Finding apparatus all belie each other as we bellow along through the fog up the east coast. If the weather turns clear and frosty, B.C/8 and Sea Slight, then we are instantly recalled to the Base. All the bad things happen on the easterly patrol. Review your past life when you round the Pollock Rock, abandon hope when you pass the Hook and the Saltees and approach the 'bottom-right-hand corner'. Don't ever ask any of the crew of this vessel what Christmas is like off Rosslare. They know. What's more, they'll tell you.

The shining place on the eastern patrol is Waterford, and the Waterford river, though I don't like tidal rivers very much; obedient to the moon they shrink into their beds twice in the twenty-four hours, exposing vast areas of sloblands given over to spindle-legged, mean-looking querulous sea-birds. Come to think of it, I don't like sea-birds much either. They are magnificent on the wing but they are cruel and predatory and without the human qualities of the blackbird and the thrush and the robin. The capon-like 'tame' seagull is a horrid sight.

On the Waterford River is a village which I must revisit when I am a civilian again; Passage East. Imagine a child making a village out of some rather old models of French houses. Build a spacious square that calls for a café and its bright awnings. Add a harbour that actually has a bistro beside it. Hang up the nets to dry and push it all under a church-topped cliff and there you have Passage East. Opposite is Ballyhack, near which a Marine Service Shore-Detachment controlled the field of observation mines which we laid between Ballyhack and Duncannon. Some years ago a British mine washed up under the cliffs below the Marine Service post and a Leading Seaman who had done a lot of time in the Torpedo Shop and who had a passion for fiddling with things climbed down and rendered it harmless. When he got back he was told that the Mine-Demolition party of the Army Ordnance Corps was on its way so he had to go down again and replace the works.

I am typing this part of my manuscript off the coast of Clare on the western patrol and though mines are still keeping us busy the brave skillful men of the Army Ordnance Corps took, and are still taking, more risks than have ever come our way.

As one approaches Waterford the river becomes more and more like the Seine. It narrows and becomes steep-to on the Port hand, then it turns dramatically – exposing Dunbrody Abbey – and suddenly Rouen lies before us in the guise of Waterford City, with brightly painted and irregularly shaped houses backing the broad quays and another Sotteville-les-Rouen forming on the opposite shore. Our berth is usually opposite Reginald's Tower, which is associated with Strongbow and Eva. 'She,' a C.P.O. once said, in a lecturing tone, 'was A Miss MacMurrough. Her friends all called her Eva but I never knew her well enough. Be that as it may they waded through seas of blood to the altar and when he had killed half the population of the city he became more Irish than the Irish themselves.'

I like Waterford very much. Its people are agreeable and intelligent, the two qualities do not always go together; it has many cinemas, a Woolworth's, an Art Gallery, a Museum (I believe), many really beautiful shops, and music flourishes there. At night some of its dark and retiring lanes and closes seem a fit setting for an Edgar Allan Poe story. In all this the citizens have a considerable amount of pleasant and proper pride.

Most of my visits to Waterford have been made during the crisp weather of early winter, with the mists massing the rising roofs into harmony and making the lights gleam more brightly and turning into a graceful engraving the great bights of electric cable which hang from tremendous pylons athwart the river. Even above the city the river is still tidal and navigable, a fierce tide which sometimes calls for the greatest skill in ship-handling.

Between Hook Point, at the mouth of the river, and the Saltees, comes Crossfarnoge Point. What does that mean? I am using the Admiralty spelling. Again and again I have found the Irish names, even in their Admiralty versions, to be helpful. To-day, in the mist, I was not quite certain which of two points was one marked Aillidie Point on the chart until I saw that one was backed off into a sharp cliff. And what could be more self-explanatory, when one gets beneath the spelling, that Birtrabuoy Bay?

Rosslare to Dublin is a dreary run until Co. Wicklow comes up, just a matter of picking up and passing buoys. If we were close enough I always had a word with the Coast Watchers on Wicklow Head by semaphore. Then comes Bray, heralding gay Killiney with its bright little boxes of houses; and then Dalkey Island, and the sun catching the windows of Howth.

'Channels' now, for the Dublin men, for the smoke of the Pigeon House is showing up over the arm of Dun Laoghaire and the Poolbeg is bathing its portly scarlet belly in the sunset, like our Chief Engineer after a swim. Now the buoys and now the Liffey; the hundred-ton crane and the gas-holder, and somewhere in the city's haze is O'Connell Bridge and the bus to home.

But first, the Alexandra Basin. The *wording* Alexandra Basin, an advantage to any city, but what a place to pass time in and, somehow, when we got into that Basin it seemed very hard to get out again. In 1941 we went to Dublin for a short dry-docking. The night before going into dry-dock we got so badly battered against another ship in a south-easterly gale that our stay had to be extended. When we got out of dry-dock a Greek broke away in another gale and wrote its name on our counter. When all that was made good we were held up again to have Degaussing gear fitted; and that wasn't the longest stay we made there.

In the summer of 1943 An Taoiseach boarded us in the Basin. It was during manoeuvres and we were just about to go out on some exercise with the First and Second Flotillas. Some army observers were expected and as I stood on the bridge setting out charts I noticed a civilian striding confidently up the gangway.

'How amazingly like Dev,' I thought, looking down to see that the man on gangway-duty turned him back. Next moment the confident civilian was on the bridge and I was saluting An Taoiseach. He was immediately followed by Mr. Oscar Traynor, the Minister for Defence, and it was quite a time before the spectators from the army showed up.

Maybe we were wrong, this is only what we thought, but our impression was that the head of the Government and our Minister had escaped for a short holiday. Though there were important Army and Marine Service men on board it was with the likes of us that Dev and the Minister mostly talked. We were asked to identify places on the chart. We were asked about the compass. We were asked about the ship in general, and Dev asked awkward questions concerning the moments of the wind about the mainsail of a schooner going down the river ahead of us. Though they were no strangers to other ships of the Service this was the first time they had been aboard the *Muirchu* as a Marine Service vessel. I suppose both An Taoiseach and the Minister were unconscious of the rather glowing impression they left on us.

That day was further distinguished by a fairy god-motherly act on the part of the Army. It happened like this.

Colonel (with his case in his hand): 'Have you got any cigarettes?'

Myself: 'I only smoke a pipe, thank you, sir.'

Colonel: 'I said "Have you *got* any cigarettes?"'

Myself: 'I'll see if can get some for you, sir.'

Colonel (controlling himself): 'Have you got any cigarettes for your crew?'

We had no cigarettes, and up they came from Cork; two thousand strong.

Mr De Valera's black hat had a tough passage of it. As it was a warm summer day he put it aside and, with such a crowd on the bridge, a seaman should have been told off to guard it. I put it on the chart-table and it kept falling off. The top of the binnacle would have supported it nicely but that would not have had a very seamanlike appearance. For a time it was hanging on one of the starboard telegraphs but a sudden ring astern on the port telegraph sent it flying again. Yes, it was even walked on accidentally. I thought of putting it in the Chart Room but imagined he might need it again, and quickly, because there was no

An Taoiseach, Eamonn de Valera on a visit to the Marine Service Depot, 1942. Note the hat.

breeze and the Poor Farmers' rather poor coal was sprinkling the bridge with soot; what happened to the pillow-cases in Blackrock that night, we wondered.

In the *Muirchu* I never went further up the coast than Rock-a-Bill Lighthouse, there we once picked up a little Danish fishing-boat which appeared to be taking fish illegally. She was the cleanest and best-kept fishing-boat I have ever seen, with a crew of three; beautiful quarters in the bows, a hold of fish and ice amidships, and the wheel-house and engines aft. We took her to Dublin. She was so small that we might as well have thrown her back. 'Vaat you think now?' was the question the crew put to us gloomily every hour or so: it became a catchword on board. We got permission for the Danes to go ashore under escort for the evening in Dublin. We told them about the original Danes of Dublin.

'We steal your fish. You gif us drink. Happy people. All mad.'

Their case was dismissed. I wonder whether you and the *Tut* have been able to return to Denmark yet, Skipper Chris Isakksen?

But the Western Patrol, ah! No need of bullock's hearts to cheer us up when we cleared Roches Point and started making up for the Old Head of Kinsale. Maybe the weather ahead would be tough, it often was, but the Western Patrol compensated for everything and from the moment we got outside the coast developed, but developed gradually as is fitting for a prelude to the glories of Mayo and Donegal.

We once crept into Kinsale with the engines barely turning after burning out twenty-one firebars, and didn't it blow that night! We would have been on a lee shore if we had been caught out. But my best memories of Kinsale are concerned with the regattas which they hold there with grace and imagination. We took the racing boats overland by lorry and slept in the military post, an old Workhouse – and haunted too, they said. The Committee did everything they could to entertain the Marine Service and the crowd was all over us when the blue and white singlets came tearing down the river to carry off the Junior Challenge Cup.

West of Old Head of Kinsale lies Galley Head and after that those savage rocks, the Stags. To my knowledge there are at least three groups of rocks so named; the Stags of West Cork, the Stags of Broadhaven and the Stags off Donegal. Many places round our coasts have identical names. I have referred to the Haulbowlines, there are also three Clogher Heads, two Bray Heads, two Bills, three Lemon Rocks – very close together, Two Mutton Islands, five Blackrocks, two Conduff Heads, two Monkstowns – and how many Black Heads?

Near the Stags is Baltimore, once sacked by Algerine pirates, its entrance guarded by a white beacon called Lot's Wife and, on the other side, by a most useful low-powered light. The anchorage off Sherkin Island (where Father

Lamb always makes the Service welcome) is mainly good, except when a southerly gale blows straight through the entrance to the bay.

On one such winter night I was called with the word that we were going out. A cup of tea, a message that the engineers were ready below, and we were off – passing the Lighthouse and Lot's Wife and plunging into the seas. When we turned eastward she put up a superb performance, I stood in one wing of the bridge trying to keep the chart and other things from sliding away and when I looked at the other wing I could see Lieutenant White away below me; next moment she would roll away over to port and I would see him holding on above me. With rain and darkness and breaking seas it was a dirty passage, filling the alleyways and keeping the decks awash. When we got past the Old Head of Kinsale and brought the seas a little abaft the beam the old man said 'I'm glad that's over.' It was the only comment on bad weather I had ever heard him make. He also asked me one time during that passage whether I felt sea-sick and when I said I was all right he stated, 'If you're not sick now you never will be,' and I recalled a furious old woman shouting to me in the pitching saloon of the Aran steamer, 'Those that are never sea-sick are never healthy!' then she hung her head again over the basin which had come cruising back to her across the linoleum.

Further west is the Gascanane Sound. Is there any derivation from 'cursing' here? Was it named so by angry mariners trying to negotiate the sound west of Badger Island? Going east to the Sound, keep the tip of the West Calf in line with the edge of Little Goat Island until the beacon on Copper Point sits on the end of the East Calf. Then alter course for Badger Island and, when the Sound opens, go through the middle of it. I learnt this, as I learnt everything else, from the old man, entering the details of each of the many troublesome little places we met on our various courses in a small book after seeing him take the ship through with calm and certainty. Don't alter course until Bird Island is open; keep off the Bullig Shoal – further than the chart shows; Clogher Rock under the tower on Sybil Head clears Stromboli; always get a four-point bearing from the Ballard Tower, if you can. It was a creed which I set all my mind on learning.

Going through the Gascanane usually meant up to Schull for mails, or going to Crookhaven. Crookhaven is now one of my chosen places which I shall visit again. I wish I knew more about it. *Sheila II*'s owner told me the story of the towers and the ruins and the old days of Crookhaven at breakfast on board one morning. I urged him to write it and I have forgotten all about it now, save that it was once a very important harbour. The entry is narrow, a fjord. One side used to be wooded, it is a quarry now, and on the other side the little village huddles down beneath the hill which shelters it from the outer sea.

We bought a goose in Crookhaven one Christmas-time. The boatswain said that he had known that goose for fifteen years, that it used to come to meet him, that it lived on fish and spoke Munster Irish. It was killed on board, I don't know how. All I know is that it was done to death on the bitts in the well-deck and that night I found a note on my pillow when I came off watch.

> please tell L/S Logue to pluck the goose.
> J. Longmore, Steward.

At the head of Crookhaven is a cockle beach which the Chief and I used to visit with buckets and a boat's crew. Gathering cockles at low water by moonlight in winter meant that one's hands were warmer in the water than out of it. But the reward! – the cockles *nature* eaten on the point of a knife, the curried cockles, the cockles boiled with a tin of tomato soup and the mussels taken from the mussel rock.

'Put a handful of oatmeal in the water,' the Chief would instruct the Steward, 'and they'll shed all their dirt.' But somehow, we never had the cockles and the oatmeal at the same time.

[Print is faded here, Ed.][Not?] Unlike many men of his imposing size, the Chief Engineer has an imposing appetite.

'That will do until lunch is ready,' he will say at the end of a meal, and if it has been a good one he will mildly remark, 'Do you know, I don't feel a bit hungry.' After lunch he will talk expertly and with authority about food he has eaten unless the two other officers are reminiscing. Then he may tell us about the barmaid in Belfast who asked him what density he ran his boilers at, or about how and where he black-leaded his Glasgow landlady.

'What is Palm-oil chop, Chief?' I once asked him at lunch. The Chief Engineer put down his knife and fork and was quite silent for a moment or two; he seemed to be praying to all the palm-oil chops he had eaten in the past. 'Palm-oil chop, Norris,' he said, at last, 'is God's greatest gift to man in the way of food. It is the most beautiful dish you could imagine being set before you – it contains *everything*! Yams, there's chicken, there's pork, all kinds of vegetables, eggs, there's fruit, there's meat, there's fish, oysters – and all cooked in palm oil.'

I could see it swimming before me.

'Palm-oil chop,' said the Chief, softly, lost in a West African reverie. Shortly after that he went for his siesta.

'... and don't get me out of bed for anyone less than the Chief of Staff.'

With such a place as Crookhaven in easy peace-time reach of Cork I can't see why a yachtsman should spend his time racing round the legs of course instead of sailing out of these delectable places and returning each weekend to pick up his small cruiser and find another port.

Beyond Crookhaven lies Mizen Head and Berehaven in Bantry Bay. It is an island which forms a fairly sheltered anchorage. The eastern end of the island is a fort garrisoned by the Coast Defence Artillery, below the fort is the village of Rerrin and the anchorage at Lawrence Cove.

One winter night we were patrolling without lights until we started to round the eastern end of the island between Lonehort Point and the lighthouse. Then we switched on and the fun began.

Instantly an Aldis lamp in the fort challenged us and one of our wireless operators replied with our lamp. Shortly afterwards he complained, 'He keeps sending O.L., sir. That means Open Your Light and mine's as bright as it can be but he still keeps on sending O.L.' O.L. may mean 'Open your Light' in the Signals Corps – where that operator came from originally – but at sea it means 'Heave-to, or I will open fire on you'; an awkward situation for us because we were between the light-house and the shore and there was a strong wind and tide.

'Get him by wireless and tell him we are coming in to shelter,' said the captain. At that moment the searchlights pounced out, catching us as we went Easy Ahead to keep off the shore. The lamp continued its pale blink of O.L. and I repeated our identity on our own lamp.

'He orders us to heave-to and will not receive any further wireless messages,' the operator was back again. Still we crawled ahead. The lamp spoke again from the fort, in very slow morse, as to a beginner. 'You-have-had-your-last-warning-we-are-now-going-to-open-fire.'

We could hear the steel shutters in the machine-gun emplacements slamming back and knew that the big guns were trained on us too.

'Go for'ard and anchor,' said Lieutenant White.

As we came up on the forecastle head in the blaze of the searchlights I thought; they will take us for the 12-pounder's crew closing up to the gun and will fire on us at once.

'Let go!' The cable rattled out and she was soon brought up. There we lay in the searchlights until the examination vessel came out to us.

There was correspondence about that episode. The point was that there was no official evidence as to what we were. It reminded me of a time when I issued rations from our stock to the *Isaalt*, the training vessel. The complexities of A.F 295A, the ship's Ration Book, was one of my cares as Chief Petty Officer and I said good-bye to it when I was promoted.

'You can't just sail about giving away food to any ship you meet,' I was told by Finance, in Dublin.

'But she's one of our own ships.'

'Really? I can't find her here – no, she's not in the official record.'

'We've only just got her. We took her over in November and she was going to Cobh in company with us and they were short of rations so ...'

'Oh, we know all about that, but we've no *official* knowledge of it. As far as we're concerned you've been giving away food to civilians. Please explain and state how you propose to adjust,' said the lady, with a charming smile.

Please explain, and state how you propose to adjust; that was very familiar phrase to me, countered by 'Clerical Error Corrected in next month's 295A.' That meant that I had made one more elementary blunder in my work. Finance knew it too, and I knew they knew it, but with a little juggling it would appear to be all right on paper, and paper was what counted. Every C.Q.M.S. does the same juggling at the end of the month and in addition to my Marine duties I had the headache of C.Q.M.S.-ing the ship.

Another headache was Income Tax. Every year Finance took back almost a third of my pay. I looked it this way; the Government pays me to act in the Defence Forces; the Government then takes back nearly a third of my pay so as to be able, next year, to part pay me to act in the Defence Forces and to then take back nearly a third of my pay so as to be able, the year after that, to part pay me to act in the Defence Forces and to then take back nearly a third of my pay so as to, etc, etc, etc. In addition I paid Civil Income Tax, so that the government might have money to add to my part-pay. Consequently I am really almost paying myself.

Maybe someone understands what I am talking about.

★ ★ ★

The funny thing about Berehaven was that if we went there on manoeuvres it was always raining and blowing but if we dropped in there on patrol the weather was usually good. They had a saying about Hungry Hill which rises on the opposite shore; 'If you can see Hungry Hill then it's going to rain. If you can't see it then it is raining.'

In Bantry town, at the head of the bay, the people always made us welcome as we poured into the town during manoeuvres. Glengarriff, Adrigole, Dunmanus – the bay is edged by lovely places. I came on watch at eight one perfect summer morning when we were entering Dunmanus Bay, it was something hushed and wonderful, to be remembered always. The sea had a faint rainbow skin stretched over it. The mists turned to dazzling silver in the East until the sun got a grip on them and slowly drew them up from the sea, baring the desolate mountains. The lovely morning was all our own. What a pity we were going up the bay just to destroy another ugly mine.

Muirchu in Berehaven.

Now it is as if the first movement of the patrol westward runs without a break into the *andante* of Kerry, for we are passing the Bull, Cow and Calf, unless the old man has taken the ship through the Dursey Sound where, I swear, it is possible to touch the rocks on the port side with a boat-hook. The Calf is the smallest of these three islands and it still carries the stump of the lighthouse which stood there, and the curved roofs of the keepers' dwellings cowering into crevices in the rock. Years and years ago a sea snapped the lighthouse off, drowning all but one man, and another light was built on the great Bull Rock which is pierced by a huge natural arch. Now our courses are well north of west and the patrician silhouette of Puffin Island shows up, with the Lemon Rock making what might be the tip of a protruding belly and the Skelligs forming the splayed feet of a stone man lying in a bath of the cosmic Atlantic bulges. There is a very unusual description the Skelligs in *The Dance of the Quick and the Dead* by Sacheverell Sitwell.

Valentia is another stopping place of ours for rations, mails and pay. The Boatswain often tells how the ship, the press and the news cameramen waited for Air Marshal Balbo's armada at Valentia in the nineteen-thirties. It was then that the puppy Balbo, who was to become the Casanova of all spaniels, came on board. The Garda Siochana band was there, too, and played nightly in front of the hotel. But, says P.O. McKeone, the local people did not enjoy the band. What they wanted, he says, was:

Dee the diddle-daddle
Diddle-dadddle-diddle
Dee the diddle-daddle
Diddel bloody day

Valentia often meant a chance to run up to Cahirciveen, where there are fifty-two public houses and though most of the shop-fronts are sombrely coloured, an increasing number of them conceal plumbing, H & C and bathrooms. This seems to be typical of Kerry towns, the Victorian is giving place to the latest from Patrick Street and Grafton Street. This 'latest' may not last like the outmoded mahogany, but what a contrast to what lies outside; the remoteness, the sadness, the almost other-worldliness of Kerry. It seems to be the answer of this bright and intelligent people to their dreamy surroundings; and I am not forgetting Waterford when I say that the Kerry people are surely the most intelligent people in Ireland and that their women are the most beautiful.

There is a cable-station in Valentia Island and another on the mainland at Waterville, a lovely place with a horrid name; why is its Irish form not more generally used? The story goes that one night the Valentia doctor was wanted urgently in the island but happened to be in Waterville, five or six miles away. It was, I believe, a matter of a few minutes, and of mutual courtesy between the two cable-companies concerned to flash the message to New York from Valentia and from New York back to Waterville, and the doctor.

To reach the Blasket Islands from Valentia one crosses Dingle Bay. (From Cromwell Point set a course for Slea Head and when the Tearacht is clear of Inishnabro steer for the tower on the Great Blasket until you open your marks for the Sound, so ran my Creed.) The village on the Great Blasket appears quite unexpectedly when one is bound up the coast; snug-looking houses with tarred roofs straggling up the hillside from where the black curraghs are ranged above the little landing-place. Further up, the water foams round grinning tuskers of rock and Stromboli lies in wait below.

'Not such a hot performance,' said Lieutenant White, suddenly appearing on the bridge during my first effort at going through the Blasket Sound, southbound. Little episodes like that stamped the coast very clearly on one's mind.

The far end of the Sound is dominated by Sybil Point, a horrifying eminence on top of which the Coast watchers signalling to us looked like toys. Below the sea has fashioned the rocks into the likeness of three nuns at prayer.

Now the broad shoulders of the Great Brandon rise to the mists which trapped more than one aircraft during the war. It is now topped by a radio-beacon. The dangerous bay leading to Fenit opens before us and we can see fateful Bannow Strand.

We were in Fenit once for five days and the people gave us presents of onions much as the Hawaians [sic] present the *lei*, and with as generous intention.

I have never seen such onion cultivation. We had lunches, teas and suppers of onions, onions, onions; fried onions, onions boiled and onions raw, onion-omelettes, onion-salads, cheese and onions. Some got indigestion but they could not stop eating and I found no ill effects from augmenting my nightly cup of cocoa with onions and cheese immediately before turning in.

After Kerry Head the country suddenly flattens away behind the Shannon estuary. I do not like the Shannon, up to Limerick anyhow. I don't know why I don't like it but the tidal Shannon is my Doctor Fell. Limerick was very good to us during a short visit in the summer of 1945. It is full of important aeronauts and here-to-day-gone-to-morrow travellers – and it oozes beautiful blonde spies, or maybe they are Limerick girls. I would say that Limerick is our Lisbon, but I still don't like the Shannon. Yet I recall a magical evening at the house of a man who had left the Service, when three of us from the ship watched the great river sliding by and saw the bats wheeling over it and the light dying on the hard hills of Clare.

Sometimes we stood close to the land but we usually made a long course from about the Brandon to the south island of Aran, with the Cliffs of Moher losing all their terror when seen from seaward, whereas Dun Aengus, in its grim resistance to the tremendous Atlantic, and the great bastions of Dun Aengus repeated in lesser degree along the islands, seems to gain from such a view.

From a small boat the Twelve Bens of Connemara are usually visible long before the Aran Islands, which do not really disclose themselves in their correct disposition until one nears them. This is the prelude to the deep bag of Galway Bay, with fishing boats working along the north shore and, maybe, the *Dun Aengus* plodding in from the islands.

After the *andante* of Kerry ending in the marshes of the Shannon Estuary comes the *scherzo* of Galway, Mayo and the islands; the *scherzo* of pleasant evenings spent ashore including all themes previously heard with a domi-nant melodic thread of the dark and still creeks round Carraroe and the rocky fields and the rising blue hills. A *scherzo* of yacht-races and horse-races and MacNamara's cellar. A *scherzo* of my own Connemara hooker shouldering the seas aside with her tarry Phoenician bows on the way to Aran.

At one time our patrol only extended to Loop Head. At the Loop we did *iom-puighidh thart* back to the Old Head of Kinsale and *iompuighidh thart* again to the Loop until the bunkers ran low. The *Fort Rannoch* carried the patrol northwards and it was in her that I learned something about the coast north of Cleggan. I had not been north of Cleggan in any ship.

Recently we met the *Fort Rannoch* at sea.

'Dry-landers!' they jeered at us, because they had been out for three weeks and we had only just come out. Someone, in a terrifying voice, added the obscure threat, 'Wait till Nellie catches you!'

I was only relieving in the *Fort Rannoch* and I was not there for long but I enjoyed my time a lot. In bad weather her motion is very violent, she is a 'stiff' ship unlike the slow and premeditated roll of the *Muirchu*, which makes one feel that an extra half-penny or even an extra match in one's pocket would be sufficient to turn her over. Several times when I was leaning over the chart-table in the *Fort Rannoch* the man at the wheel had to sing out to me 'Watch yourself now, sir,' in an instant she had shipped a big one and flung herself away from it.

Since there seemed to be no constant differences between her Steering and Standard compasses it was necessary to climb up to Monkey Island and use the voice-pipe to steady her on a new course or to take a bearing unless, for the latter purpose, one tried the deck-head pelorus. I used it several times with reasonably accurate results but for ease in manipulation one might just as well try to play the trombone in a very small lavatory.

The journey to Monkey Island was slow, especially at night. First one lifted a grating in the wheel-house (watches were kept there, or on the machine-gun bridge below) and climbed down a ladder. A few lurches brought one past the wireless room and down another ladder at the bottom of which a third ladder led one straight up to Monkey Island. My first ascent was about ten miles

Fort Rannoch and M.T.B. *M.3* in Foynes 1940. Note 'Monkey Island', where the compass is on top of the wheel house.

off the Aran Islands to seawards, with a strong following wind pressing me against the ladder and blowing the fumes of the funnel over me. One final heave brought me over the top and as we whistled from side to side in a good lump of a sea I felt that the heroes of the old sea-stories, who went to sea as boys before the mast and were wont to lay out along the yards with only a foot-rope for support, were no worse off that [sic] I was, though I admit that I was railed in. Steadying her on a new course was simple, but getting a Fix or an Error was harder because it meant struggling to get the top off the binnacle and then taking care that it was not blown out of one's hands. *Brown's Nautical Almanack* for this year shows me a picture of a sort of periscope arrangement which will probably do away with the trips to Monkey Island. On the journey back there was a good chance of stepping backwards straight down to the stoke-hold if the fiddley had been left open.

My first sight of Donegal Bay was when coming on watch again at Noon, after that dark night. Perfect! A bright sky with great puffs of cumulus, a warm Sun and white-flecked seas tumbling onwards towards the faint coast-line which, at the end of the day, hardened into the hills of Donegal as we entered Killybegs and anchored there.

We had come straight from Berehaven, thirty hours steaming, and Killybegs, with the tumbling green fields surrounding it had a hard, bright precision which made a contrast with the less-defined scenery of West Cork. In fact it reminded me of a landscape target; 'lone bushy-topped tree', 'road-junction', 'hedgerow', 'gable-end of house', – they were all there, set out in the very colours used by the artist who designs these military vistas.

The *scherzo* is over and Donegal is the finale of the last movement of this symphony, if the changing and developing coast can be likened to a symphony. Rounding Rathlin O'Beirne [sic], everything takes on grandeur; towering Slieve League and Arranmore; lofty Muckish hiding its pigs back in the clouds; splendid, shining Errigal; sinister Bloody Foreland and wild Horn Head. Wild as Horn Head is, the weather, sea and mountains seem to combine into one magnificence, into one thunderous splendour, and the movement ends with broad closing chords *largo e maestoso*, passing inside Tory and entering the calm serenity of Lough Swilly.

★ ★ ★

I don't know what the attraction of the sea is. It would be hard to explain why a man goes to sea, apart from seeing foreign ports, but it something more than a matter of a sea-faring job being as good as any other job.

The sea is unique. There is nothing one can do for the sea. One can take the ordinary precautions of seamen against it, or build a breakwater against it, but one can do nothing for it: the sea, blindly, does all that is done.

The land is different. It can be drained, manured; keep it in good heart and it will reward you. Not so the crawling sea. It strikes and destroys without passion, it is calm and smiling and beneficent without volition. Its apparent fury is a matter of balance between air-pressures. The Sun and Moon together give it motion, the Sun warms it or chills it according to its declination.

It is always man against the sea, never the passionless sea against man. The very fish that swim in it are more sentient than their terrible element. Seafaring is a struggle against a thing without even the most elementary instincts, a thing absolutely unevolved, blind and crawling. Every voyage is an achievement against the unconquerable and as surely the ship's wake is smoothed away so surely will the struggle be renewed, and always differently. Perhaps that is what draws men to trafficking in little or high degree with this unseeing one, this insensate one, this blind and crawling sea.

13

Slow Ahead

In my chapter on the Depot I described a walk back from our Mess to the ship. If I had not known what was really going on behind the facade of undisturbed routine I might have felt complacent about things, but as I walk past the billets I know that great spaces of them are now still and empty. A derisive little notice has been stuck up in one of the windows by someone: 'Flats to let. Apply to The Army.' Men are being found with difficulty for maintenance and guard duties, already I have said good-bye to fourteen men in our crew and there are more to go.

For the crowd is breaking up. Long ago we got rid of some men. Later on men who were urgently required back in civilian life were released. Time went on and they began to go in twos and threes; now they are going in thirties and forties.

What can one say, can one blame them? No, a man who has a job to take up in civilian life can't be blamed for applying for demobilisation or transfer to the Reserve of the Service he joined for the Emergency, especially while places are being held open for those who served in the Defence Forces.

But what inducement was offered to these men to stay on and make a career of the Marine Service? And the bitter truth is that no inducement whatever was offered.

In the spring of 1945 all ships' companies and Depot personnel were paraded and addressed by army officers. The first one recapitulated how the Southern Command had taken over the administration of the Marine Service.

'When you came down here you were unwanted children,' he said.

'So now we're a shower of bastards,' muttered voice in the ranks behind me. He also said that if we tried very hard we might come up to the standard of good soldiers, though with our standard of intelligence (for which we had been hand-picked) our military attainments should be higher than those of a first-class private.

Well, that left the Marine Service feeling a little puzzled. Then a second officer began to talk. He started by reproaching us for a lack of *esprit de corps*. *Esprit de corps*! We had it all right, and now the solid anger set in. In spite of the dual-control of the Service we were firmly loyal to it and our comrades. In spite of the army regarding us as soldiers in sailors' uniforms, in spite of the lack of understanding of our requirements and of the essential difference between soldiers and sailors, in spite of the control which over-rode our own officers – in spite of all this we stood up for the army if we ever heard it adversely criticised. A third officer said that he had nothing to add to what had been said. This episode occurred at a time when there was a great hope running through us that our service was going to extend and that we would achieve independent control and be run by seamen.

All right. So we'd no *esprit de corps* hadn't we? We marched off glumly and broke up into angry groups after being dismissed. No one ever criticised the way the army ran itself and our relations with the soldiers, as individuals, were usually good. Supposing a senior Marine Service officer had addressed the assembled troops in Collins Barracks and reproved them for being deficient *in esprit de corps* ...

That morning's work did untold harm.

Later in the year an Army Form was distributed among the Emergency Men telling them how they could re-enlist for Permanent Service, transfer to the Reserve or obtain their Discharge. An Army Form; the fact that it was an Army Form and that it referred to Privates, Corporals, Sergeants and others, instead of to our ranks, caused deep distrust. Surely a little imagination could have been used? Surely a Marine Service Form could have been drafted in order to give us some idea that the Service was not going to disappear from the sea? No, it was with an Army form that men sat down in forecastles and billets to talk the whole thing over and to consider their futures. *Esprit de corps*, and no evidence that the *corps* would not be completely swallowed up by the army, for the whisper began that if one re-enlisted one could be transferred into the army against one's will. This was strengthened by a paragraph which, in effect, said that a man would be liable to serve in any branch of the army. The next said that, as far as possible, men would be kept in their own branches of the army. It was army, army, army and the Service didn't like it, and the more it was talked over the less the Service liked it. They came to us and asked us what guarantee there was that they would not be transferred to the army if they re-enlisted – what guarantee there was that there would be a Marine Service at all. And we could not answer them, we knew as little as they did, but passed on the enquiries to higher quarters.

For weeks we lived on the usual rumours and then came the memorable day when – oh, incredible statement –it was officially announced that the betting was that the Marine Service would continue, but maybe it wouldn't; and would we please tell our friends?

That finished it. Men who had applied for discharge but who, even so, thought they might re-enlist if the prospects were good were now, finally decided. Those who were hesitating previously now applied for their discharges.

A few, stayed firmly on. And so we Regulars watched the breaking up of those who had made the Service with us.

And then we were asked to encourage the men to stay on. They didn't laugh; they were polite, sorry, firm. No more sailoring under soldiers for them.

Naturally there were contributory causes to this breaking up. There were empty promises, there was the promotion of some men over the heads of others whom we deemed the better men, and there was the disappointment of those who joined up hoping to go to sea and found themselves on general duties in the Depot. What could a man in such a position say to his friends? A soldier is in a different position, but when a man puts on a sailor's uniform he becomes surrounded by what is known as 'the romance of the sea' and his friends ask him what ship he is in, and where he goes, and what he does. Many of our lads in order to keep to the truth would have to say, 'I stack turf, I pick grass off the Square, I wash up in the Seamen's Dining Hall.'

Again, this is lack of imagination, of putting oneself in the place of a seaman in the Depot. These fatigues I mention must be performed but, retaining key-men on board, the rest of crew could be switched to the Depot while Depot personnel took a turn at manning a ship.

Every time a seaman came from the Depot and stood before me while I entered his name in the Crew Book I felt that here is a man who has escaped and who has succeeded in doing what he joined up to do. Even if a man only came to replace a man on leave, or in hospital, even if the time he spent with us was at anchor, he was in a ship and he had s ship's name to put at the head of his letters. That small matter means nothing to those in authority but it means everything to a man whose friends at home regard him as a sailor. I hated losing any man back again to the Depot and in five years I can only recall two cases of men who were discontented on board.

Lack of definite information about anything gnawed at the patience of many a man and all the rumours were eagerly listened to. If the rumour has been pleasant and then turns out to be false, or just fades away, then the discontent is increased. We had no real confidence in our Administration Building, instead of being the beginning and end of all control over us it was really just a link between ourselves and the Southern Command. How well we knew the answers; Command hasn't given a ruling yet ... Command would never

Sanction it ... your case hasn't come back from Command yet ... Command wants further data.

It was the late President Roosefelt [sic] who made press conferences famous. At these conferences he told the assembled reporters what they wanted to know, or as much as he was able to let them know – and a lot more 'off the record'. The Press then passed the President's answers on to the world. How much better this is than suddenly pulling a *fait accompli* out of a fog of conjecture. How much better if a responsible officer had told us 'The future of the Marine Service will be discussed at a conference in Dublin in two days' time. In four days I will give you news of how things are going. The questions which you have asked me will be brought up at the conference.'

Too simple to work?

A man who has joined the Defence Forces has taken on a hard life but he is still a thinking individual who is entitled to be kept aware of how things are likely to be with him. Probably the Army Form was quite satisfactory for the soldier but a little consideration would have devised another one for the sailor.

Yet the army could be courteous and considerate. The army encouraged Rugby Football, holding that a man who had given up his civilian comforts should not have his sports interfered with. Another example, a personal one. I was on a Course in 1940 during the season of lent. A Mission was being held in the Barracks and all men were confined until seven o'clock each evening. I walked down to the gate and was just going to turn away when the Military Policeman called me and showed me one solitary name out of the eighty of my unit. It was my own name. I was the only Protestant on the Course. I had not sought permission to be excused from the restriction. My name had been sent down on a special Pass Roll for one man, a matter of thoughtfulness and courtesy somewhere. I never forgot that to the army.

Why wasn't there more of that? Why was coldness and impersonality allowed to break up our trained men?

★ ★ ★

And so I am walking back to the *Muirchu* from the Mess after a very strange evening.

Except for a few of us the Ante-room was almost empty. We were sitting near the fire, Nick Kennedy, myself, a young Leading-Seaman who was leaving next day and a couple of others. The number of those who would be left to us by Christmas had just come out and we were feeling bad about it. Half-laughing and half-bitter we were trying to make out what the future would be. The men had been let go without a word. There was a handsome gratuity to

come but there was nothing so heart-warming as a word of thanks spoken to
them. Their Discharge Books would follow shortly, Army Discharge Books –
fine reading for a ship's officer when one of them applied for a job. The trained
men were being let go and recruiting was to begin. There were not enough men
to man our ships and yet rumour said we were getting more ships. There was no
sense in it. We started talking of men who had gone already.

'Damned shame the way he was treated – don't know how he stuck it so
long,' of one.

'It broke his heart leaving to-day, but what else could he do,' of another.

'The best worker we ever had on board, he'd have made a first-rate
Leading Seaman.'

'... and a man with his experience too. He could have run rings round
anyone in Seamanship.'

'Yes – but maybe he couldn't throw the proper number of grenades into the
rings,' and bitter laughter again.

'Do you remember in Collins Barracks, Dublin, how we used to think ...'
began Nick. Yes, we remembered. We remembered how we had taken stock of
each other, and the wild drive south in the open lorries. We remembered the
early days in Haulbowline when we were actually building the Service, even
by such humble jobs as whitewashing and scrubbing. We remembered the new
M.T.B.s coming and we remembered the recruits who joined us in the Depot,
the first Emergency Men, the crowd we took in hand before we were properly
organised ourselves. Somehow that draft seemed to stamp themselves on us
and we had a particular affection for them – our first recruits. Then more and
more recruits had come. And these were the lads who were being let go now
and no one tried to improve their conditions or to offer them a new deal. Oh,
monstrous!

To break up such a company, for when any body of men is banded together
and dedicated to a good purpose society must be the loser by their dissolution;
each man is a part of the life of his fellows and it cannot be good to disperse
such friends.

I am so proud of the Service, sometimes unreasoningly, sometimes in just
looking at a boat-load going ashore, sometimes in seeing all the ensigns lowered
together at the Lawrence Cove anchorage during manoeuvres. Clean, friendly,
grumbling, laughing, confident and capable in their jobs – these men who built
up the Service can never be completely replaced. For me they can never be
replaced at all. I know that others will come along and they, too, will be trained
up to be seamen (and not soldiers specialising in the sea, one hopes), they will
fill the empty ships and the ships that are coming, but for me they will never
be the same as the men who came up voluntarily in the threatening times and

who united in making the Service the shining thing it was. I will not say that I will never forget them. Remembering and forgetting refer to things past but the Service will always be present with me and from time to time I will wish that I had this man or that alongside me to speak to, to lend a hand, or to be advised by.

So, as we sat by the fire and spoke of all we had hoped for and all that had come of it, our group, in the way things happen, seemed to cohere – united by a common anger.

And suddenly the young Leading-Seaman who was leaving next day, and who had been quite silent, said, 'Ah, well, I'll sing you a song.' It was so completely unexpected and so entirely wrong that one knew it was the perfect thing to happen, and the beautiful air began.

> My young love said to me 'My mother won't mind
> And my father won't slight you for your lack of kind'
> Then she stepped away from me, and this she did say
> 'It will not be long, love, till our wedding day.'

The short waves splashed loudly on the slip outside.

The new order. The arrival of the corvette *LÉ Macha* marking the transition from Marine Service to Naval Service, 1946.

She stepped away from me and she moved through the fair
And fondly I watched her move here and move there
And then she went homeward with one star awake.
As the swan in the evening glides over the lake.

Of all songs, why was he singing this song?

Last night she came to me, my dead love came in
And so softly she stepped that her feet made no din
And she laid her hand on me and this she did say
'It will not be long, love, till our wedding day.'

After that we broke up and went to our various quarters. The whole evening
ran over in my mind as I walked back to the ship. Why had he chosen that song,
why had he sung of the brightest of all hopes taken away? In the separation and
darkness of death?